NOT ALONE

NOT ALONE

By

EUNICE V. PIKE

MOODY PRESS
CHICAGO

To
My Sister Sally

Contents

Preface

"WHAT'S YOUR NAME?" a little Mazatec Indian girl asked me.

"My name is Eunice. What's yours?" The little girl covered her face in shyness and confusion. She was glad to know my name, but she had no intention of telling me hers. She turned to her companion for counsel, and I heard whispering noises coming from behind their shawls. Then they came to a decision and the shawls dropped back to their shoulders again. Her eyes twinkling, the little girl answered firmly, "My name is the same as yours. My name is Eunice."

Almost all Mazatecs are hesitant to tell their names. Their reason is this: if one man wishes to harm another, he hires a witch doctor. The witch doctor, supposedly, has the power to converse with demons, and for a price he will transmit the man's request. He will ask them to cause the enemy to have an accident, or to make the enemy or his family ill. The demons are paid for this service with turkey eggs, parrot feathers, or cocoa beans which are buried in the ground for their use.

But, according to the Mazatecs, even after the demons have been notified, they cannot carry out their assignment unless they know whom they are to harm. The Mazatecs believe that the demons can learn the identity of an individual only if told his name. Following that logic, any person who succeeds in keeping his name a secret cannot be harmed by a witch doctor. Because all strangers are believed to be witch doctors until proved innocent, those Mazatecs who count themselves susceptible to witchcraft will do their utmost to keep their names from newcomers. From their point of view, the really clever thing to do is to turn the witch doctor's evil design back upon himself, and that is why I have so frequently been told, "My name is Eunice!"

I don't intend to harm the Mazatecs, nor even to frighten them, and knowing how distressed they would be if their names were to be printed in a book for all the world to see, I have given the Mazatec characters of this book, and the towns in which they live, fictitious names. The incidents told about them and about us are all true, however.

So much has happened since I went to Chalco in 1936, that three years of those experiences have almost filled this book. I couldn't bear to stop, however, without giving some of the more recent news. Therefore, the last chapter hurries through to the spring of 1953. Some day, in another book or two, I hope to tell more of the details of those years from 1940 to 1953.

—EUNICE V. PIKE

Mexico City
October, 1953

CHAPTER I

Departures

(OCTOBER, 1936)

IN THE SAN LAZARO railroad station of Mexico City venders were selling trinkets, coffee, soda pop, candy, and corn tamales. Passengers for Oaxaca were hurrying onto the train with loads on their backs, or with baskets or bags on their arms. It was almost time for the train to pull out, and co-workers of the Summer Institute of Linguistics and the Wycliffe Bible Translators had come to see three of us on our way.

As members of the Summer Institute of Linguistics, we were to investigate an Indian language and to write up a report of it. As members of the Wycliffe Bible Translators, we were to translate the New Testament into that language and to tell its message to the people among whom we were working. As members of both organizations we were to teach people to read, and to help them in any way we could.

W. Cameron Townsend, our leader, had already translated the New Testament into Cakchiquel for a tribe in Guatemala, and he and his wife knew the hardships as well as the pleasures that accompanied life in an Indian tribe. My brother, Kenneth, who had already worked a year among the Mixtec Indians, was accompanying Florence Hansen and me to help us get settled among the Mazatec Indians.

One of our friends standing at the train window was scheduled to go to the Mixe tribe, and another to the Totonac tribe. They all knew the seriousness of the undertaking, but at this time any feeling of concern was ignored, and they told jokes and made small talk. None of them mentioned that we had been called "two young inexperienced girls," and that people in general considered it unwise for us to go to the Mazatec Indians. Some people had reminded Mr. Townsend that Latin American women never traveled alone, never lived alone, and were always well chaperoned. With genuine concern for Florrie and me, they had said that any attempt on our part to live in an Indian village would be misunderstood by the people and could only end in disaster.

I glanced at my partner Florrie, the other "young inexperienced girl." A language major and a Phi Beta Kappa from the University of California at Los Angeles, she didn't appear to be concerned about future hardships, but rather seemed to be looking forward to an encounter with the Mazatec language.

My own alma mater, Massachusetts General Hospital, had prepared me for public health nursing. Our friends said that we should make a good team, for Florrie could do the language work and I would help the people. As a graduate nurse among a primitive people, I would do marvelous things, they said. I wondered.

Ding! That was the bell, the first of three that

signified the departure of a train in Mexico City. Our friends crowded closer to the window. This one offered a last bit of advice, and that one checked to see that we had all our baggage.

Ding! Ding! The second bell. Our friends stepped back, but continued to call in whenever they could think of a remark suitably frivolous.

Ding! Ding! Ding! The train moved. "Goodby!" Mr. and Mrs. Townsend passed out of sight, but several of our pals walked beside us, then ran, and then—they were gone.

I turned from the window to see what the people were like who were traveling with us. Most of them were well-dressed, for we were traveling first class. Most of them, too, had black hair and dark complexion, and this made Florence's blond head stand out conspicuously. I listened as the people talked, and tried to pick out and understand even one word. I couldn't, and I wondered if I ever would. To me their voices seemed high-pitched and excited, and my head throbbed with the unintelligible noise.

I looked out the window hoping that if I ignored the people my headache would stop. It didn't—there was no getting away from the clatter, but the scenery was interesting, anyway. From Mexico City our trip was taking us south, past the two snow-capped volcanoes, through the city of Puebla, through the city of Tehuacán, and down into the State of Oaxaca. We had left Mexico City at five o'clock in the afternoon, and although our destination was only about 250 miles away, the train would not arrive until after midnight. We hadn't been under way very long, however, when the conductor came down

the aisle inspecting the tickets. When he looked at
ours, he was concerned.

"But nobody gets off there!"

Well, he was almost right, for certainly no Americans got off there—that is, no ordinary Americans
did. But as Bible translators we had to go to a people needing the translation. Because the translation
had already been done for most people living in
easily accessible places, we were going to a people
back in the mountains, a people with no modern
means of transportation.

The conductor still appeared doubtful at half-
past two in the morning when the train stopped and
he shouted, "San Martín!"

I had been watching for the place, but even with
the train stopped I could see no sign of a city or
even a town. We got ourselves and our baggage off
and stood beside the tracks while the only light in
sight rattled away.

With flashlights extinguished but in hand, Florrie
and I remained with our belongings while Ken went
exploring. San Martín turned out to be little more
than a railroad station, but Ken found a man who
was willing to drive us to the town of Tepetlán.
We loaded the baggage into the back of his truck
and climbed in after it. Riding backwards in the
dark, jouncing, bumping and being bumped, we
traveled about half an hour before stopping beside
a building with a big barnlike door. The driver
honked his horn, and Ken knocked loudly. Finally
the door opened a crack, then a little more, and a
woman, holding a candle high above her head, in-

vited us in. We were tired, and her comfortable beds were very welcome.

In the morning Ken arranged with a man to take us on to Chalco, and that afternoon the man and his helper arrived with donkeys. We had a heap of supplies—kerosene, gasoline, canned milk, canned vegetables, army cots, clothing, books—and it took at least an hour to tie them on the donkeys.

It was five o'clock that afternoon by the time we left with the three riding and eight pack animals. The heat of the day was over and the country was beautiful. Ahead of us, as far as I could see, was range after range of mountains, and here and there a trail disappeared in the distance.

The animal I was riding was a small horse, and he didn't like associating with donkeys. If one came close to him, he bared his teeth and dived for him. As long as it was light I didn't mind that he kept ahead of the pack, but later I wasn't pleased to be in the lead. After dark when I could neither see Florrie nor Ken, my only connection with human beings was the whistle with which the animal drivers urged their animals on. I had never thought the whistle of a strange man could be a comforting sound, but that one was.

We stopped for the night in the Aztec village of San Fernando. It had an inn which had more room for the donkeys that it did for us. Ken slept on the counter of its little store, and Florrie and I had the bedroom. The bed was a board shelf built out from the wall, with a straw mat laid over the top— no covers, no mattress, no pillow. As we rolled up in our blankets, I heard the animals munching their corn outside, and then, almost immediately, I was asleep.

We were up early the next morning, but it was eight o'clock by the time the last animal was loaded and we were plodding on our way. Because none of of the animals wanted to be last and therefore within reach of the driver's whip, there was a continual jostling for position. Except, however, for the occasional sprint that the jostling necessitated, the animals hardly changed gait. Their pace was slow, the distance far, and we had plenty of time to think over what meager information we had about the Mazatec tribe.

In Mexico City we had searched the records of the Mexican Department of Statistics, and had learned the names of the towns in which the Mazatec-speaking people lived. By putting a check mark on the map over each of these towns, we had located the general region of the Mazatec tribe. We had put our finger on one of the larger towns of that area, and had made our plans for living there, without knowing much more about the place than the information we had received from the census book— "population 1,775; altitude 5,800 feet."

The drivers had told us that we would not arrive in Chalco until three in the afternoon, but as we traveled we kept our eyes on the mountain ranges ahead. We hoped, if only by a glimpse from the distance, to increase our knowledge of the town that was to be home.

At last, across a deep valley and to the left, we saw a town. "Is that Chalco?" we asked the driver.

"No. Chalco is far."

An hour or two later we saw another group of houses; again they were to the left of us. "Is that Chalco?" we asked.

"No, lady, Chalco is far."

Still we traveled, and then about two o'clock in the afternoon the man pointed. "Over there. That's Chalco." We looked across the valley to a mountain range ahead. Below us, for that mountain was not as high as the one we were on, was Chalco. A few clouds, white against the green mountainside, covered part of the town, but even so, compared to the other villages which we had seen a few hours before, Chalco was tremendous.

We didn't comment, Florrie, my brother, and I, but we studied the village until the trail dropped behind the range again. Later the trail rounded another corner, and again the valley was before us, and this time the man did not have to point out our destination; we saw for ourselves.

For about two more hours we squirmed in our saddles and tried to relieve our knees from the ache of the long, seemingly endless drop to the river. The water's roar as we approached was welcome, for it indicated that the bottom of the valley was near. We crossed over a log bridge and then slid back in our saddles as the trail started up. What a relief! On the downgrade I had braced my feet in the stirrups. Now on the upgrade I took them out one at a time and swung them back and forth. It both hurt and felt good to move again.

That last climb took us about an hour. We were too close to see the town any more, but any number of signs told us that we were approaching a village.

We passed a cow or two tethered in the field, a corn patch, a bit of sugar cane. Later as we neared a hut, dogs barked, a little child cried with fright. Older children, too, ran at the sight of us, but came back again to peek at us from behind the house. Their feelings were similar to ours—we were curious about the people of the town, but a bit afraid to arrive and take up life among them.

By five o'clock, with a crowd of people watching from a distance and others following, we were entering the main part of the village. The driver guided us to the town hall, and the journey was over. I climbed off, staggered, and hung on to the horse. He was a good old horse, but I hadn't expected to hug him good-by!

While Ken went in to greet the mayor, a crowd gathered and made the most of their first opportunity to study an American. The mayor, as in most Indian towns, wielded tremendous power. He could give us a place to live—or drive us out. Ken showed him our official papers, and requested that we be allowed to stay in the village. He gave his consent and came out to meet Florrie and me. Helpfully he offered Florrie and me a room at one end of the school building, and Ken one on the second floor.

The driver had been waiting to find out where to unload. Now, at a word from the mayor, he took the animals down to the school and piled our luggage on the floor of the assigned room. The people followed us, packing the doorway, and even crowding into the front part of the room.

We needed supper and a light to work by, and to get them we opened some of our boxes while the people watched, fascinated at the sight of things they were seeing for the first time. We got out a gasoline lamp, kerosene stove, the army cots, and sleeping bags.

The room was big, and while we stayed at the further end of it the people were quiet, watching, talking softly among themselves, but when I started toward the front of the room, there was a shriek from the children and a stampede toward the door. I went back to the other end, and they slowly pushed in again. (And these were the people whose language we were supposed to learn!) The next time I smiled as I went forward, but it did no good —they still shrieked and ran.

We wondered how long they'd stay; we were hungry, but almost too tired to eat. Most of all we wanted a chance to rest and to be alone. Darkness was our friend in that instance, for at dusk the children left, and a little later the men followed. At last we could shut the door and go to bed.

When we opened the door in the morning, the children walked in again. Our room next to the school gave them a wonderful opportunity to learn firsthand some of the habits and customs of Americans. The room to the left of us was the post office, and across the yard was the church. If we had expected to stay only a day or two, we would have enjoyed the excitement and the chance to watch while being watched, but since we were looking forward to five, ten, fifteen years in the town, we wanted a chance for privacy.

The next day, in search of this privacy, we moved into two unfurnished rooms, part of an adobe building owned by a family named Sánchez. The house was located on "main street," the one part of town that had electric lights—from six to ten every evening. For a short distance the street was paved with cobblestones, and on both sides, running from one end to the other, were shops and stores.

Most of these were "grocery stores" selling sugar, salt, chili, candy, macaroni, canned salmon, matches, soap, and cigarettes. In addition to these supplies, the Sánchez' store had aspirin, castor oil, Epsom salts, hydrogen peroxide, and a few toilet articles. The "department stores" sold cloth, blankets, shawls, ribbons, buttons, and thread. Sometimes in one store and sometimes in another there were nails, string, kerosene, lamps, and dishes. Just across from us was a bakery, and here and there throughout the town were little places that sold liquor, soap, matches, and cigarettes.

These stores were supplied by pack trains that came in from Tepetlán, and when they arrived on Tuesday, Thursday, and Saturday, the street was crowded with mules and donkeys. On these occasions I held my breath whenever I made my way through the traffic, past the heels of this mule and around the nose of that one, for I wondered if one of them might not nip me with his radiator, or deflate me with his back tire!

Although Chalco was twenty-five miles from the nearest road over which a car passed, and although it seemed to us to be a mere country town, it was the economic, political, and cultural center for the Mazatecs in that section of the tribe. Chalco itself, spreading out across the mountainside, covered an area of about a mile and a half at the longest part, and a quarter of a mile at the widest. From a distance the town hadn't looked so big, because the dried sugar-cane leaf roofs and the unpainted board walls had blended in with the earth of the gardens or were hidden by the leaves of coffee trees.

It was the coffee bean that brought money into the area; and because of the coffee, land meant wealth for the Mazatecs. Land was also used for corn—the staple of Mazatec diet—but the people did not have a surplus of corn, instead they imported it between seasons.

A few people made money in carpentry, and although the item most in demand was coffins, they also made chairs, tables, window shutters, and doors. They did not keep furniture on hand, however, and because it usually took them a week or two to fill an order, Ken bought secondhand furniture for us: three chairs, a kitchen table, and two other tables for desks. From the boxes our supplies came in, we made cupboards. We bought still more boxes and made dressers for our clothes and shelves for the kitchen. Another box Ken turned into book ends, and the top of the kerosene can became a dust-pan.

As long as Ken was busy, he was willing to stay with us; but now that the house was in order, he began to get restless, thinking of his own work among the Mixtec tribe. Florrie and I knew that he'd have to leave eventually, but we also knew that something unforeseen might arise that would be hard for us to handle alone.

Even while he had been setting up the house, he

had taken a few hours each day to help us with the language. Rufina Sánchez, our landlord's daughter, was our official teacher, but the whole family wanted to take part. They gathered around and listened with delight as we repeated words after her. Rufina wasn't really a teacher; she was an "informant." She didn't plan the lesson as a teacher does; rather, we were the ones who planned it. She merely sat there, answering whatever questions we asked her.

One day we happened to ask for the word "pig," *chinka,* and then Rufina volunteered the word "shirt," *chinka*. They were alike except for the pitch of the second syllables, and Rufina repeated them with delight, for she knew that such words were hard for the Spanish-speaking people, and she expected that we would react against them too. We did. Right then Ken urged us never to forget that tone made a difference in the meaning of words, and to continue our study of the language with that fact in mind.

Ken filled those days with bits of advice; he helped us not only on language study, but he instructed us on life in an Indian village, hoping to anticipate situations which might confront us after he was gone.

On October 28, about five o'clock in the morning, the three of us walked down the trail over which we had traveled two weeks before. At the river an hour below the village we stopped; then Florrie and I turned around and walked back up the trail, and Ken crossed the river to the other side. As Florrie and I climbed one mountain, we looked across the valley and watched Ken climbing another. Step by

step he became smaller in the distance. As he neared
the ridge, he turned, and we could make out his hat
as he slowly waved it from side to side. A few more
steps and Florrie and I were alone—but not alone,
for the Lord was with us.

CHAPTER II

Linguistic Beginnings

(OCTOBER, 1936 — MAY, 1937)

MOST OF THE TIME we studied, although only
an hour or two each day was spent with the informant. Rufina gave us new words and sentences, and
helped us perfect the pronunciation of words we
had already acquired. We practiced until we could
say with a minimum of effort sentences for greeting
people and sentences for shopping in the market.

Frequently the people laughed so hard that they
neglected to answer when we said "good morning"
to them. They laughed not because we had pronounced the words incorrectly, but because they
were startled that a stranger should speak their language at all. When they realized that we were trying, most of them had an irresistible desire to check
up on us. That desire was realized by some of the
women almost every time we went for water.

Because there was no natural spring at the village
center itself, water had been piped in from a spring
a mile or so away. The water trickled slowly from
one outlet, and the women had to take turns filling
their jars. It was while we were waiting our turn
that they quizzed us. They didn't believe that it was

possible for us to learn their language, but they thought it a big joke that we were trying.

"What is this?" they asked impudently.

"Nose."

"What is this?"

"Eye."

"What is this?"

"Stone." The only break in their questioning came when they took time to mimic our mistakes; otherwise the examination continued from the moment we arrived until we were on our way home with a full pail.

Vocabulary had always been one of my weak points, and the effort to remember words under those trying circumstances exhausted me. I was glad when we were able to hire a girl to get water for us. Rufina Sánchez was in too high a social class to carry water. She didn't even keep the teaching job very long, but as soon as the novelty wore off, she gave it up to an orphan girl by the name of Marta. Marta worked with us all day long, carrying water, washing clothes, and acting as our language informant. She spoke only Mazatec to us, and even though it put drastic limitations on our conversation, we spoke only Mazatec to her.

Almost every afternoon the three of us took a walk together, and Florrie and I increased our vocabulary by listening as Marta answered our questions of, "What is that?" When we saw traveling merchants arrive, or pack animals coming in from the trail, we pointed to one of the animals and asked the usual question. When the answer was "donkey," we felt that we had understood, but there seemed to be two words for "horse." Marta would not let us interchange them; so we watched to see to what kind of animal she applied each word. Pack horses and riding horses? No. Dark and light horses? No. Old and young horses? No. Big and little horses? No. Then one day I noticed the creature's ears. "A mule!" I shrieked, and so it was. Florrie and I may not have recognized a mule when we saw one, but Marta did.

We had learned to distinguish mules from horses, but that was just one of the many nonlinguistic things we found to be closely related to language. Our eating was related to linguistics, in that we bought our food from people who spoke only Mazatec and our contact with them was made in that language. Of course, there were other problems involved—the lack of refrigeration, for example. Because we could buy meat only once a week, we ate meat two days a week and eggs the other five. Wanting a little variety, we asked Rufina about the possibility of buying cheese, and she told us that it was sold in white round cakes. On market day, we looked for it and bought three nice white patties. My mouth watered at the sight of each piece wrapped so nicely in a clean green banana leaf.

The next day we planned to have cheese for dinner, and as the medical books said that cheese sometimes carried malta fever, we decided to sterilize it by cooking. I started to cut off the outside, and was surprised at how hard it had become. Apparently it had dried out very quickly—how thick was that outside part, anyway? I called to Florrie and asked for her opinion. We were still puzzling over our

problem when Rufina and her sister Silvia walked
in. We held out the patty and asked, "How do you
prepare cheese for cooking?" Our question seemed
to perplex them; so we asked, "You don't eat this
tough outside part, do you?"

Then understanding came, and with it a shout of
laughter. They tried to explain, but their words
were distorted beyond our recognition, and it was
some time before they had quieted enough to tell
us that our white patties were not cheese, but lime!
The people used it to soften the hull of their dried
corn. Before being sold in the market, the lime was
dampened and shaped into patties about the same
size of the round native cheese. When we were in
the market, the little round cake had still been
damp, and of course we had not called for it by
name; we had merely pointed and asked for "that."

Even when we did know the name of the article
we wanted to buy, the problem of mathematics still
faced us. Typical was the time we tried to buy
eleven eggs, all the woman had, at four centavos
each. Forty-four centavos for all, we figured, and
handed her a fifty-cent piece. The woman wiped it
with her handkerchief to be sure it was good, bit it
for the same reason, and then held it up for her
neighbors to see. She knew we had change due us,
but she didn't know how much; so her friends
gathered around to help her. They put the eggs
into three little piles of three each, with two left
over; and then they put them back again, looked
puzzled, and smiled uncertainly. We wanted to tell
them to give us six cents change; in fact, we tried
several times, but either they didn't understand, or

didn't agree. Finally I gave the woman a five-cent piece and took it away again. That seemed to satisfy. She took out a handkerchief, untied the money in it, and handed over all she had—three centavos. We took it, glad to end the scene, even though we considered that six centavos would have been the correct amount of change.

Actually, because the Mazatecs still used the old Spanish money system—one bit equals twelve and a half centavos, two bits is twenty-five centavos—the correct amount would have been five centavos. According to Mazatec custom, the woman would have sold one egg for four centavos, two for eight centavos, three for twelve centavos; but for six eggs she would have demanded twenty-five centavos. Twelve eggs would have been fifty centavos—that is four bits. It was a week or two before we came to understand that type of mathematics, and our teacher on the latter occasion was an angry woman who thought we were shortchanging her.

In other situations children were our teachers, although from their point of view they were merely looking at magazines or playing games. The game, "Pick-up sticks," was a favorite with them, and they got as excited about it as people at a football game. The manufacturer in his printed rules had said that only one stick was to be moved and picked up at a time. He had also said that each person should play from one spot at the table, without infringing upon the other fellow's territory. The Mazatec children played on the floor, and no mere rules hindered them. Round and around they went on elbows and knees, with the head, left arm, and shoulder guarding the pile. Only the right hand was used to pick up the sticks, for if the player relaxed his guard and tried to use both hands, the other children, with complete disregard for the rules, helped themselves to a stick or two. The player's protesting cry as he tried to complete his turn was what taught me "Wait a minute! Wait a minute!"

As unconsciously as the children had taught me that phrase, I found myself teaching the Sánchez girls English. My purpose was to teach Silvia to tat, but I didn't know enough of either Spanish or Mazatec to tell her what to do with her hands; I had to place them in position and demonstrate what should be done with the thread. We had worked most of the evening, and as Silvia made a loop of her own, our concentration was broken by a peal of laughter from Rufina.

When I glanced up, she said to me in broken English, "finger."

Then I realized that as I had been helping Silvia I had been chattering along in English. I tried to stop, but I couldn't—my tongue had to wag to match my fingers. By the time the evening was over, Rufina had picked up the words "finger," "see," and "now."

My English gave the Sánchez family pleasure on another occasion. One day while I was calling at their house, the prettiest little puss walked into the room. Immediately I snapped my fingers and called, "Kitty, kitty, and kitty." The cat never moved, and as I gave up I realized that Rufina and Silvia were watching me with interest and amusement.

Then Rufina stuck out her lips and in a kind of hissing whistle called, *"Pachootee, pachootee, pa-*

chootee," and the little puss pricked up his ears and miaowed.

At that moment I realized how completely different my Connecticut world had been from the one in which I found myself at the time. I started right then to practice that *pachootee* hiss, for I knew that I would never feel at home until I could at least call a cat.

I learned dog language too, but the knowledge didn't make me feel at home, probably because at home I had never chased dogs from the kitchen. In Chalco our kitchen had a door but no window. We kept the door open to get light—and got dogs too, for they smelled the food and sneaked hopefully in. As we cooked we learned to keep half an eye on the door, and when a dog stepped over the ledge we said, "Pssst!" All but the most stubborn immediately ran. The stubborn ones sank to the floor in an effort to become invisible and didn't move again until they heard the Mazatec for "Get out!"

We never succumbed to the temptation to use that dog language on human beings. Curiosity brought them through the door, and seldom were we without an audience. One time I counted fourteen people watching me prepare dinner. The egg beater was the biggest attraction, for the Mazatecs had never seen a machine like it. Sometimes children ran at the sound of its roar, but returned when they realized that it did no harm. Pepper was unknown to them, and when I told them that it was something like chili, they wanted to taste it and make the comparison for themselves. The kerosene stove interested and perplexed them—they could hardly believe that a blue flame could be hot, and one little girl passed her hand through it to find out. Because their food, cooked over wood, tasted of wood smoke, they were sure that ours must taste of kerosene, and occasionally they expressed their pity that we had to eat it.

A meal without onlookers was restful but infrequent—even our evening meals were watched. We usually ate supper after dark and with the door closed, but, beside the outside door, there was a door that went from our kitchen to the Sánchez store. That door had a knothole in it. Every evening after we had shut the outside door, an eye appeared at the knothole of the other one. First one eye and then another peeked in as the customers made the most of their opportunity. The hole was seldom vacant until the family closed the store for the night. We didn't talk to the eye; we pretended to ignore it, but it was there. Then one afternoon, a child, eating an orange in our house, stuck a piece of orange peel in the knothole. Florrie and I were elated—the orange peel would stop the peekers and we'd have an unwatched meal at last!

Evening came, the outside door was shut, the lamp was lit, and as we glanced in appreciation toward the orange peel, a finger came through from the other side and knocked it out, and an eye took its place. The watch continued, not for that night only, but for the entire year that we continued to live in that house. Of course, we could have nailed a board over the hole, but—well, maybe if we let them look long enough, they'd get over their distrust of us.

For the most part I had only one escape from that tiresome watched feeling, and that was through my letters home. The contact with people who understood and appreciated the purpose for and use of teakettles and toothbrushes was a restful one, and letter writing became a relaxation. Of course, I occasionally detoured through Webster to find the spelling for a word, but that was nothing compared with the frustration that came with knowing the exact word I wanted to say, but at the same time being incapable of putting that word into the language of the person to whom I was speaking. Therefore, even though the mail came into town only three times a week, it made up an important part of Florrie's and my life. We looked forward to its arrival and always had letters to send.

One day, because we had been a little late finishing our letters, it was half-past seven and dusk when we walked down to mail them. When we reached the post office, the door was shut; but because a light was on inside, we thought that we could still give our letters to the postman. We knocked and then heard voices but no one came. We knocked louder, and when still no one came, we tried again, louder still. Then we heard the key turn and stood back, and it was a good thing we did, for the gun that was thrust through the open crack wasn't many inches from our stomachs as it was. When the man holding the gun saw us, he was embarrassed, poor fellow. He tried to hide the gun, but it was too big for his pocket. He could not hold it behind his back, keep the door open, and take the letters we were handing to him all at the same time. His stammered explanation was that we had not answered when he asked us who was there. On the way home, Florrie and I decided that if the postman's reaction was typical, we would stay in after dark. We liked to have our letters go as soon as they were written, but, hereafter, unless they were finished before dark, we'd wait and mail them in the morning.

We could be sure that each mail day would bring us some mail, for we had ordered a daily paper from Mexico City. Because it was in Spanish I didn't read it much, but I found good use for it. Placed between my sleeping bag and the army cot, the papers made a good insulation against the cold. They crackled the first few nights, but as they were broken in, the crackle left them. In spite of the fact that both Florrie and I used the newspapers as mattresses, we had a pile of extra ones; so one day I made a hat from one and placed it on the head of a six-year-old boy. "Now you're a soldier," I told him, and he went out, proud and happy. I grinned and wondered what my public health nursing friends would have thought of that hat, for it was merely an oversized trash bag, the kind we pinned to the patients' beds.

Within five minutes the boy was back with three of his brothers who wanted hats too. Those four little boys were just a beginning, for immediately other little boys flocked in. An hour later there was a lull in the business, and I stepped to the door and looked out. Twenty-five boys with newspaper hats and sticks for guns were joyfully parading the street.

Again I grinned as I thought of my nursing colleagues—and then I stopped. Here I was, a much-touted nurse, graduate of the Massachusetts General Hospital, trained in public health nursing, and what of all my acquired knowledge had I used in making friends among the Mazatec Indians? Simple. I had used my knowledge of trash bags. The people hadn't had enough confidence in me to ask for much medical help. I had dabbed a disinfectant on a few scratches, bandaged a stubbed toe or two, but all the medical treatments put together had not made the friends that those trash bags had.

That night every time I turned over in bed I thought, "trash bags." One minute the ridiculousness of it almost made me chuckle, and the next minute Isaiah 6:8 seemed to echo through my mind. Isaiah had told of his vision, and how the Lord had said, "Whom shall I send, and who will go for us?" I had always supposed that my answer had been the same as Isaiah's, "Here am I; send me." Now I wondered; perhaps the answer had really been, "Here am I; use my nursing." Who was I to insist upon what the Lord should or should not use? It was plain to be seen that I was no judge of what was useful and what was not.

A shed tear or two at the trash bags, and then, "All right, Lord, if You can find anything else that's useful, You may have it." And my answer to His question became more like Isaiah's, "Here am I; use me."

Nursing and nursing thoughts, as the days went by, became shoved to the background, and language study and its analysis took their place. To supplement Marta, we hired Carmen an hour or two every afternoon. She spoke Spanish as well as Mazatec, and her help speeded up Florrie's work with the verbs and their tenses. For the most part, I continued as I had before, conversing in Mazatec, and only occasionally did Carmen change and tell me the meaning of a word or phrase in Spanish.

With my limited vocabulary I sometimes, much to the amusement of my informant, had to use gestures to express my ideas. At one time I tried to find out what in Mazatec corresponded to English adjectives or adverbs. My feet always being with me and handy, I started walking. As I walked I asked, "What am I doing?" She told me and I wrote it down. Then I walked faster and asked again. I walked slowly, then stopped, then sideways. Carmen, through her giggles, gave me the sentences I asked for. She even managed to say something when I tried to walk bowlegged, but she never did control her hysterics enough to give me a word for pigeon-toed. That word remained to be discovered.

On less exciting days, Carmen went to sleep. She, who could wash clothes and grind corn hours at a time, tired quickly with the mental exercise of language study. When she became sleepy, she leaned forward and rested her chin on my desk, her arms dangling at her sides, and her eyes shut. When I asked her a question, if she answered at all, the words were distorted by her closed teeth. I could understand her distaste for language work, but if I had to spend two hours at the desk, I wanted to accomplish something by it. One day the closed eyes, the tightly shut teeth, the delayed answers, became unbearable. I jumped up, pulled her off her chair, chased her around the room a few times, rolled her on the floor and chased her some more. She came back, giggling and puffing, sat down in the chair, and gave me the best lesson I had had for weeks.

Even when Carmen stayed awake, however, her mind was frequently not on the job. One day I was studying expressions of time, trying to determine their meanings and when they were used. I wanted to hear a group of sentences in which the noun and verb remained constant. If I could recognize the noun and verb each time, then any change in the expression of time would be more apparent. For that purpose, I gave Carmen a sentence in Spanish and asked her to translate it into Mazatec. The first sentence was, "The girl sold beans." The next, "The girl sold beans for the first time last Sunday." Next, "The girl sold beans in the market frequently." In each of those sentences I could pick out "girl," "sold," and "beans" without difficulty. Then, "The girl had sold beans since she was a little girl." "The girl sold only a few beans today"—but when Carmen translated that sentence into Mazatec, I couldn't find the verb "to sell." I knew of no reason why it should have dropped out, but I suspected that Carmen's mind had wandered. In order to check up on her I read the Mazatec sentence back to her and asked her to tell me its meaning in Spanish.

Her answer was the same as my request had been, "The girl sold only a few beans today."

I had her repeat it for me in Mazatec, but I was still unable to recognize the word for "sold."

Almost in protest at my own density, I objected, "But which is the word for 'sold'?"

Carmen looked startled as she asked, "You said that she had sold beans?"

"Yes."

"Oh," she explained, "I said that the girl bought only a few beans today."

I might keep her physically awake by tickling her, but the only guard against her mental sleepiness was to increase my own alertness.

Florrie seemed to be alert to words not only during the language lesson but in other situations too. I was less so, but when I could pick a new one out of the air I was very happy. There was the time that Florrie went to market while Marta and I were studying upstairs. Usually the downstairs door was locked unless we were in the kitchen, but that morning Florrie had merely pulled the door shut behind her. A little later I heard it open and called, "Is that you, Florrie?"

"Yes," she answered. Marta, always anxious to pick up an English word or two, asked, "What does 'yes' mean?" I told her and she asked, "How do you say, *ania?*" I had never heard that expression before, but as she had said it pointing through the floor at Florrie, there was no doubt but that she was saying either, "It's me," or "I'm here." From that hint I was able to get, not only "I am," but also "you are," and "he is."

Even the discovery of new words did not stimulate me for long. I couldn't stand to think Mazatec all day, and so late every afternoon I relaxed with a two-year-old girl and her three-year-old sister. They were nieces of Rufina and Silvia and lived across the street from us. At first when I tried to play with them, they just stood and stared at me, but after we became friends we had a good time together. I forgot all about Mazatec and Spanish and talked good old Yankee to them. Sometimes people passing by saw us, and they watched in amazement, for they themselves couldn't understand what I was saying, but they saw the little girls respond. With awe the onlookers said to each other, "They understand English!" and I believe they did.

CHAPTER III

"Where Is She?"

(June, 1937 — January, 1938)

IN JUNE Florrie and I prepared to leave for the States, where we would attend another session of the Summer Institute of Linguistics. When we told our Mazatec friends that we were leaving, the almost universal comment was, "You won't be back." When we insisted that we would return, the answer was often a laugh and the one word, "Liars." We had already stayed longer than anyone had imagined we would, and our explanation that we were going to school seemed to them to be only an excuse for leaving. They had seen any number of outsiders come, stay awhile, and then leave forever, and that was the conduct they had come to expect from schoolteachers, post office personnel, tax collectors— and us.

Only the Sánchez family realized that we meant what we said, and it was not our words which convinced them, but the fact that when we left our belongings were stored in their house.

Knowing the attitude of the other Mazatecs, we hated to delay our return when the summer session was over, but we postponed it again while I took a semester at the Moody Bible Institute. I enjoyed

the classes, but the day after they were over I headed
back to Mexico. In less than three weeks from the
close of the semester, Florrie and I were back in
Tepetlán, the town in which the road ended and
from which we rode horseback to Chalco.

Florrie and I were no longer strangers in Tepetlán, and the people of the hotel gave us news of
our Mazatec friends. They told us that Luisa, the
mother of my two little playmates, had died. She
had needed medical attention, and because there
was no doctor in Chalco, her husband had brought
her out to this town. In spite of doctor's care, however, she had died the same day that Florrie and I
had arrived there.

Although we were not too sure of our Mazatec
etiquette, Florrie and I decided that we should at
least go to the house with our sympathy. We put
on our nice dresses and walked up the hot, dusty
street. It was hard for me to realize that we were
passing individually owned houses, for a continuous
adobe wall lined the sidewalk. The only indication
of separate ownership which I could see was the
pink, blue, white, and tan paint with which different sections of the wall were painted. The doors
were wide, heavy, and of a kind that could be barri-
caded securely. The windows were spacious, but
covered with iron bars. As we passed by the open-
ings, we could see comfortable rooms, courtyards
with flowers and birds in cages, and stables with
animals and dirt.

Unusual activity around a section of wall warned
us that we were approaching our destination. Some
people, seemingly busy, were hurrying in or out of

the door. Others, with time on their hands, were just loitering there. As we entered and went on to the parlor, Old Mary, Luisa's mother, threw herself across the room into Florrie's arms. As she sobbed, she wailed, "Where is Luisa? Oh! Oh! Where is Luisa?"

Well, where was she?

Her corpse was lying on a table at the end of the room in front of an image of the Virgin of Guadalupe. Between the image and the corpse and on both ends of the table, candles were burning. Calla lilies and other white flowers were filling every otherwise vacant space. Again Old Mary wailed, and the sound didn't stop in my ears or head; it ripped down through to my heart. She was right. That dead thing wasn't Luisa. Where had she gone?

We stayed a few minutes, sitting with the other women guests on the benches that lined the wall of the parlor. As we sat there, I looked—I hope without staring—and saw that everything not pertaining to the funeral had been removed. Except for the benches, the flowers, the guests, the corpse, and the knickknacks of religious significance, the room was empty. Beyond, in the kitchen, several women were working hard and fast, for theirs was the job of preparing the funeral feast—turkey, chili sauce, tamales, coffee.

The church service and the burial took place the next morning, and we had intended to go, but, perhaps because they knew that our religion was different from theirs, the family neglected to tell us the time, and Luisa was buried without us. It was apparent, however, that they appreciated our friendship, for they stopped for us when they went back to the cemetery. Those closest to Luisa—her mother, her husband, her sister, two of her brothers, and Rufina, her sister-in-law—with a few other people were returning to the grave for a quiet farewell that could not be shared with the many who had been at the burial.

The cemetery was surrounded by a high wall, but one of the men had a key which unlocked the door leading into it. As we passed through and shut the door behind us, our view became restricted to the wall and a sea of blue gravestones. The tombstones consisted, not only of a headstone, but also of a coffin-like affair made of cement which covered the entire grave. Quietly we walked through the "blueness" to the spot where the earth was still damp.

We sat facing each other, some on this gravestone and some on that, with Juan Sánchez, Luisa's husband, and Old Mary in the center by the damp spot itself. For a moment we were quiet while several of the men lit cigarettes and the women adjusted their shawls. Old Mary began the reminiscences by telling what a good daughter Luisa had always been. Juan mentioned what a wonderful wife she had made. One by one, sometimes with long pauses in between, her relatives talked of Luisa. They spoke of things she had done, what she had said, and of those things relating to her illness. As they mentioned her illness, Old Mary became bitter—it was Juan's fault that her daughter had died. Juan defended himself—true, she had died in childbirth, but he had given her good care, he had spent money on medicine, and he had taken her to a doctor. But even as they spoke crossly to one another, they seemed close in their sorrow.

Again Old Mary wailed, "Where is Luisa?" No one answered. We sat silent around her grave. "My daughter! My daughter! Where is my daughter?" Still no answer. The sun set, the wall and the stones faded from view, and it was dark.

The next day Florrie and I tried without success to find horses and a guide to take us to Chalco. Juan heard that we were looking for animals and offered us two of theirs. Eight men had come over for the funeral; they were returning that night and were willing to slow their pace to ours. They would be traveling in the moonlight to avoid the hot sun, and if we wanted to go, we were to be ready by six o'clock.

Florrie and I remembered the concern which people had about our traveling unchaperoned, and we didn't intend to be foolhardy, but it seemed to us that to travel with men who were friends (not only Juan, but also his father would be in the crowd) was at least as safe as traveling in the company of a strange guide and of whoever happened to overtake us on the trail.

We told Juan we'd go, hurried into our riding togs, and joined the party. Six of us were riding and four were walking, but we traveled together, for on those rugged trails a man made as good time as a horse.

We were not even out of sight of the town before one of the men asked me, "Do you have a pistol?" Several of the others turned to listen to the answer.

Again I remembered the concern which friends had for us as I answered, "No."

"But don't you know that there are robbers in these mountains?"

"Yes, but with all these men, why should I need a pistol?"

"That's right," they said soberly, and pulled out theirs to show me.

As we climbed the mountain, the sun went down. For a little while it was dark, but then the moon came out, and we put away our flashlights. We could see not only the trail but down into the valley as well.

About half-past eight we reached San Fernando, the Aztec village where Ken, Florrie and I had spent the night on that first trip in. We stopped about halfway through the village and crowded into a hut. Contrasted with the bright moonlight it was dark inside, even though someone had lighted a lantern and had set it in the middle of the dirt floor.

After a while, an Aztec woman brought in coffee and bread for us all. I had never liked coffee anyway, and this was black without milk or cream, and had been cooked with brown sugar. I sipped a bit while I watched my chance. As soon as Florrie had finished her cup, I swapped mine for hers, but someone saw me and told. As one man they called for the cook. "More coffee for the *señorita!*" And so my cup was filled brimming full, and yes—I drank.

Our lunch finished, we started on again, still climbing. Tepetlán was about 3,500 feet above sea level, but the summit ahead was 8,600 feet. The trail on the Tepetlán side of the summit was considered dangerous, for that was the region preferred by highway robbers. They robbed not only the mail, but individuals as well. They wanted not only money but merchandise, and sometimes they killed their victims in order to get it. The men had been talking and joking, but as we neared the summit they became quieter. Still farther on the talking stopped entirely, and we traveled fast as the men urged the horses on.

Then for some reason two of the men became angry. They fought—but because neither one wanted to get behind the group, each managed his blows by timing them to the other's walk. I had seen men fight in Chalco with drunken screams and loud curses, and I had never been much impressed. I had walked around them and had gone about my business. Seeing the men fight here, the only sound that of fist against flesh, sent shivers up and down my backbone. Previously, I had half doubted the robbery tales, but if the men were that conscious of the need for silence, surely robbers must be close by. After a bit Juan separated the two men and with gestures threatened and rebuked them for fighting in such dangerous territory.

The summit, with deep valleys on two sides, was foggy, windy, and cold. Holding our hats and turning our heads down against the breeze, we crept across, and I was glad when we were below the crest again. The danger from robbers seemed past, and from there on the horses chose their own gait and no one paid much attention to anyone else. We traveled silently, more from inertia than intent.

All at once, from somewhere up front there was a

pistol shot, and then one behind—here, there and everywhere the men were shooting off their guns and shouting. I couldn't see any robbers, so I wondered what had gotten into them. One man slipped up and explained, "Before we were sleepy, but now we're awake."

They began to estimate the distance to Chalco and the time that we would arrive there. It was then only two o'clock, but the general opinion was that we would be in by four. The guess was a good one, for by half-past four we were actually at the outskirts of the village. The horses' shoes clanked on the cobblestone street, the dogs sent up a howl, and the racket brought Silvia Sánchez to the door. She gathered us in, and insisted that Florrie and I finish the night in her bed while she and the rest of the family slept on the floor.

The next morning news of our return spread quickly, and people came to greet us. They were glad, but surprised that we were back. "We thought you weren't coming," was the most common remark.

"We like Chalco; we wanted to come," we told them. They found that hard to believe, but the fact that we had returned backed up our statement, and they looked at us with wonder in their eyes.

On market day as we walked through the square, we heard excited whispers, "The white-headed women are back!" The name "white-headed women" seemed queer to Florrie and me, but it was in keeping with other Mazatec names. Their black-haired, black-eyed friends with lighter than average complexions they called "Blondie." Those with darker than average complexions they called "Blackie." To

Florrie and me the difference was so slight that we
had to study before we could predict who would
be "blond" and who "black," but to the Mazatec
the difference was easily apparent. In fact, although
I had black hair, the color of Florrie's and my skin
was to them so startling that a shout of "white-
headed women" let anyone within hearing know
we were approaching.

It was that shout that kept us under surveillance
when we were on a walk. The people liked to watch
us, and the children loved to greet us. To some of
them it was almost a game; they would shout,
"Hello!" and "Good-by!" as many times as we would
repeat our response.

The people who saw us most frequently were
those who lived beside the path to Marta's house.
Previously, Marta had come to our house, but because we more easily picked up household words
and phrases when she was in her own home, we
had arranged to have our lessons there. We found
that the new environment did have one disadvantage, however; Marta had many visitors; each was
filled with curiosity about us; and at intervals the
lessons were interrupted while that curiosity was
appeased.

One wet morning a young girl named Nina, one
of five guests there, made a study of my clothing.
She inspected my leather jacket—the pockets, the
belt, and the zipper. My skirt came next—how warm
it was. I was sitting with my feet under the table,
so Nina got down on her hands and knees the better
to see my stockings. Gently she tested them—how
smooth they were! When she reached my feet she

found my rubbers and her astonishment overcame any reticence she might have had. "Look, look! She's wearing two pairs of shoes!"

The other visitors hurried over, and the lesson stopped while Marta went around the table where she could see, too. Chatting excitedly, they snapped the rubbers and experimentally pulled the heel on and off. I smiled and waited until each had had a turn; then I planted my feet on the floor and took up my studying again. As the days passed, the rubbers continued to attract so much attention that I hated to wear them, and I found myself choosing wet feet in preference to rubbers and the commotion that accompanied them.

On one of the coldest mornings, there were six people in the hut besides me. With the thermometer in the lower thirties, the men were not working, the women sewing, nor the children playing. All but Marta were huddled around a tiny fire in the center of the hut. The sticks of the fire were laid out like the spokes of a wheel with the coals for the hub. The fire was at the hub, and as the ends burned off, the sticks were pushed farther in. Whenever a big gust of wind came, the boards rattled, the thatched roof sighed (something like the pine trees back home), and one or more of the group uttered an expression of disgust.

The window shutter, as well as the door, was closed, and I wrote by the light that came in through the cracks of the wall. Marta was too cold to sit at the table with me. She paced the floor as she answered my questions, and blew on her hands when she was not actually talking. Ida, a little seven-year-old girl, squatting with her knees over the fire, had neither a shawl nor slip, and I could see her shiver through her dress.

Before the end of the lesson, one of the men had to leave. As he got up to go everyone sympathized. "It's bad going," they said. "There's a lot of mud." A flock of chickens outside had been watching their chance; and when the door opened, they dodged in, squawking as they tried to escape their owner's determined feet. Their effort was to no avail, for all but one, which was allowed to stay in the corner, were shooed out again.

Going to Marta's house every day and meeting her friends and relatives helped me to feel closer to the whole tribe. Through Marta, I was beginning to see how the Mazatecs lived and how they felt, and through her the throngs of people who came to market began to take on personality. The women were a beautiful sight, with their black, shiny hair hanging down their backs in braids. Some of them wore American-style dresses like Marta's, but most of them used the colorful native costume. The tunic of the costume, reaching to the knee, had five rows of blue and pink ribbons, two running up and down and three across, and the white muslin between the rows was almost solid with embroidery. They had two types of skirts, but both were ankle length and swished when the women walked. The everyday skirt was a heavy blue and white cotton material. The more expensive skirt was white with heavy red wool embroidery at the bottom. Even the men were colorful, for although their pants were white, their shirts were of various colors—yellow, blue, pink, and an occasional green.

Every market day several thousand people came to Chalco to buy and sell. Two sheds, running the length of the square, were used by the butchers, leather workers, and drygoods-merchants. Other merchants brought tarpaulins and put up temporary shelters in the center of the square. The pace through the market was necessarily a slow one, because those who were selling a few bunches of bananas, a heap of oranges, or a pile of soap sat on the ground with their merchandise in front of them. There were so many selling and the crowd was so great that only with care could a person avoid stepping on someone's oranges or tripping over a pile of corn. In spite of the crowded condition, the people were orderly and soft-spoken, and although they elbowed their way through, they were pleasant about it. Business was brisk until about eleven o'clock, but after that there were no new arrivals, and the crowd thinned as many started home.

One market day I stood in our doorway and watched the throng stream past. On the path in front of me as well as on that to my right, there was constant movement of people. Where were they going? If I had asked them, they would have told me that they were going home. Probably none of them lived more than six hours away, and most of them would be home in less than four. But where were they going? Even Old Mary knew that it wasn't the body that counted. She had cried, "Where is Luisa?" though she herself had helped stretch the body on the table.

I thought of Luisa as I watched the crowd move past. The answer as to their destination was easy if they knew the Lord, for He had promised eternal life to those who believed. But "faith cometh by hearing," and these people, these hundreds on their way home from market, had never heard. And "hearing [cometh] by the Word of God," but the Word of God had never been put into their language. How could they hear unless someone, Florrie and I, translated it for them? Our job became clear as I watched and realized that unless these streaming out from Chalco should receive the Word and come to believe in Christ, they were among the "unbelieving" of Revelation 21:8 who would "have their part in the lake which burneth with fire and brimstone: which is the second death."

CHAPTER IV

Tone Tangles

(FEBRUARY — APRIL, 1938)

WHILE FLORRIE AND I were studying Mazatec in Chalco, Ken had continued with his work on Mixtec. Even though that language kept him busy, he didn't forget us and the problems facing us in our study. He wrote reminding us of the words "pig" and "shirt" and urging us to analyze the tone of the Mazatec language. But tone was hard for us to hear, and we still managed to convince ourselves that it was not too important.

By not taking tone into account, however, we sometimes came to queer conclusions. There was the day I wanted to get the word "thin," and so I pointed to my own face. Carmen answered, *k'en*. That startled me, because the word for "dead" was *k'en*. I wondered if Carmen considered me as thin as a dead person. If I had noticed that she had spoken that syllable on a little lower pitch than usual, I might have realized that she had not said the word for "dead" at all. She had given me the word for "pale," but I had misunderstood because it differed from "dead" only by the pitch on which it was spoken.

I occasionally tried to record tone, but listening to

it took such an effort that after ten minutes of
study I was exhausted, and annoyances which I overlooked at other times were almost unbearable if
they occurred while I was listening for tone. Carmen had always tried my patience, and during one
of the lessons that I had set aside for the study of
tone, she sat at my elbow with a head cold and no
handkerchief. The rhythmic snuff interspersed with
bigger snuffs drove any acuteness of hearing from
my head. After a while I handed her a Kleenex and
explained that it was what we used when we had a
cold. She was interested in that bit of information,
thanked me for the Kleenex, and then carefully
wrapped her fancy work in it. She continued to
snuff and swallow, and again I gave up on tone.

Soon after that Carmen stopped working as informant, and Florrie and I began looking for someone to take her place in sharing informant duties
with Marta. It was Marta who suggested that we try
Catarina, her next-door neighbor. We agreed and
went over to meet her, a married woman about
thirty-five years old. She greeted us, and then said
something which to our limited knowledge sounded
like, "Are you going to work here?"

Since we had come to make arrangements for her
to work with us, we answered, "Yes."

The shout of delight that went up from Marta,
Catarina, and the always-present onlookers told us
that our guess had been wrong and led us to suspect
the truth, even before she translated for us, "Are
you going to marry here?"

If we hadn't had our minds set to discuss work
and informants, we might have guessed her question

correctly, for it was one that was hinted at frequently. The Mazatecs expected us to marry, for we were of the marrying age (a little older than most Mazatec brides), we were still single, and as far as they could see, without parents to look after us. The question which they debated among themselves, and about which they constantly asked us, was whether or not we would marry a Mazatec. We tried to be so on the alert that no hope could arise either in the hearts of the young swains, or in the hearts of those looking for an illustrious daughter-in-law. Occasionally we slipped as we had done that day and gave the people a good time at our expense.

Actually the sentences, "Are you going to marry here?" and "Are you going to work here?" differed considerably, and among those differences was one of tone. The part which meant "marry" was low and the part which meant "work" was high.

Stubbornly resistant to the idea that the tone of Mazatec must be analyzed, we found that such incidents were pushing us closer and closer to the day when we'd have to settle down for a real try at the job.

Tone had been bothering my big brother Ken, too, as five days' journey away he worked on the Mixtec language. One day listening to the people of the village where he was staying, he'd be convinced that tone was an inherent part of the language and that it was often the only difference between words. A few days later, confused because the words frequently had different tones in a sentence from what they had when spoken alone, he would conclude that the Mixtec could not possibly be a tonal language. At one time he decided that if the same word was ever said with two different tone patterns, then that automatically proved that one was not important. With this in mind he memorized the pitch of "cloud," *biko,* and a number of other words. Then he set his mind to listen for those words in conversation; if he even once heard them with different pitches from those he had memorized, then, he thought, tone could be disregarded.

He didn't have long to wait. A few days later, as Ken was returning with Lucas, his informant, from a neighboring town, the man paused at the spot from which the distant mountains could be seen. He pointed in the direction of one of the biggest ones and said a sentence with "cloud" in it, and the pitch he used at that time was not the one Ken had so carefully memorized. Even as Ken responded to Lucas, he was struck by the significance of the incident. Now he *knew* that tone in Mixtec was incidental, and he rested in his decision.

But he couldn't rest long because the decision did not stand. Pairs of words continued to turn up which were different in meaning but which, except for tone, were alike in pronunciation. Once more Ken was torn with uncertainty. He wanted to grind out the answer, but he had no steady informant with whom to study. Lucas, even when he worked, came only a few hours each day, and he had worked only seven days that month.

One morning Ken watched Lucas approaching. Lucas' actions were strange, and he was too polite to be normal. Ken had guessed the reason even before they were within speaking distance. The man had come to work, but he was drunk—too drunk to be any linguistic help. Despair gripped Ken's heart. He wanted to translate the New Testament for the Mixtec people, but how could he when he had no one to teach him the language? How could he when the tone played tricks on him? Again and again he had tried. Again and again he had failed. He wasn't even sure that tone was an essential part of the vocabulary. He thought it was, but if so, how many tones were there? Two? Three? Four? Why was it that he heard a word one way one day, and another way later? Was his ear bad, or did the tones actually change?

Discouraged, tired, conscious of failure, not only the Mixtec weighed heavily on Ken's shoulders, but the Mazatec did too. He knew that I was baffled by the Mazatec tone, and he felt that he should help his little sister. Nor was he concerned with only Mixtec and Mazatec. Otis and Mary Leal, colleagues preparing to translate for the Zapotec people, were also puzzled by things they heard. They were asking Ken questions that he couldn't answer, and he felt that if he couldn't answer them, his failure would affect not only the Mixtec work, but the Mazatec and Zapotec as well.

Ken's most immediate need was an informant—a man to take Lucas' place. He needed someone who would come every day, and who would be in condition to work after he arrived. He had tried for months to find such a person, but without success. Now the need seemed more urgent than ever.

The next day, New Year's Day, 1938, he arose

before sunrise and started up the mountain that overlooked the village. Although he had had no breakfast, he carried not a lunch but a Bible. And although his need was for an informant, he was going, not to some village, but rather to a secluded nook among the pine trees. He found it, near the top of the mountain, a short distance from the footpath. Satisfied that he would not be disturbed by the occasional traveler, he knelt down on the soft, smooth pine needles. From a grateful heart he remembered and thanked the Lord for many blessings and for the help he had already received.

Then he took his Bible, and leaning against a tree he read of the Lord whose "is the greatness, and the power, and the glory, and the victory, and the majesty," and who is "exalted as head above all." And he read that he had but to ask and that the Lord would both hear and answer. So again he got to his knees, and this time he asked for an informant, for someone who would come regularly to study. He made other petitions, and then, tired, he lay down and slept. When he awoke, he continued in prayer, and slept again when tired.

All day long without food and without water, he praised God, laid his petitions before Him, rested and prayed again. At dusk Ken came down from the mountain and went back to his hut. As he was hunting through his supplies for something to eat, Lalo, a steady, hard-working man came in. For a little while he was quiet, watching Ken move around the room, but not for long—he soon told of his purpose for coming. He was Lucas' brother, and he knew that Ken needed an informant, and he had come to offer his services. Ken had asked him before, but he had always said that he was too busy. Now he suggested that if they studied early enough, then he could work in the cornfield afterward. Arrangements were made, and Ken went to bed rejoicing and remembering that the Lord had said, "While they are yet speaking, I will hear."

Every weekday of the month that followed found Ken and Lalo at work by 5:00 A.M. Lalo was a better informant than Lucas, and even though Lalo could be there only two hours each morning, Ken made progress. In his study he was following up a suggestion made by the eminent linguist, Sapir. One evening in 1937 during a casual conversation, Sapir had said that words of a tone language should not be analyzed one at a time, but rather that the analysis should be a matter of relationships—the pitch of each word should be compared with the pitch of others.

In his study with Lalo, Ken was making lists of the words which were alike in pitch, and by the end of the month it was complete enough so that he felt that he could start comparing the various lists. He hoped that with the comparison he would find the answer to the tone problem that had been plaguing him. But he didn't want to take that step alone; he had already had so much trouble with Mixtec that he was afraid he would miss the answer. He wanted the help of God who created the universe. He knew that God who at Babel had scrambled the world language could bring order out of chaos and make him to understand the Mixtec system.

Once more he made his way up the mountain and

gave himself completely to prayer. He prayed for the Mixtecs, the 165,000 of them who needed to be told of Christ, and who needed His written Word. He prayed for the 55,000 Mazatecs, and the Zapotecs, and for the tribes who spoke other tone languages which he knew should and would have translators someday. He told of his need for help—how could he translate the Bible into Mixtec if he couldn't hear and record one of the essentials of that language, tone? Desperate as he was for the answer, concerned as he was for the Mixtec, he asked that the solution not come to the Mixtec problem until with it he had a technique which he could apply to other language problems and with which he could help his fellow translators. By sunset, tired, hungry, thirsty, he felt prepared for his next two-hour session with Lalo.

The next day he listened to the informant repeat the lists of previously arranged words, and he wrote down the pitch of each one as it compared with a word which he had chosen for criterion. It was the use of the criterion word which helped him to see that the tone of speech was relative, and that the Mixtecs changed key according to their moods. By the time he had listened to the same lists several times, comparing them with different criterion words, he began to see that in some instances the tones of one word affected the tones of another. This explained why he had heard the word for "cloud" sometimes with one pitch pattern, and sometimes with another. The mysteries of Mixtec began to unfold.

One more day, that is, two more hours with the

informant, and the problem with its solution which has stood the test of years was spread out before him. It was this: Each syllable of Mixtec was spoken on either a "high," "mid," or "low" pitch, and certain words exerted an influence upon other surrounding words and caused them to change from one pitch to another.

The echo of that triumph reached over to Florrie and me. Ken wrote to us of the system which he had found, and of the importance of tone in the Mixtec language. He predicted that we would not only have vocabulary difficulties, but that we would find ourselves unable to cope with the grammar unless we understood the ways of Mazatec tone. His letters were long and full of suggestions for starting the analysis.

So I tried. It was a queer job for a nurse, and sometimes I wondered what my pals would think if they saw me shuffling the words around. According to Ken, I was supposed to put all words of like pitch together, and I worked until I had several heaps. If I could manage to get the words into the right number of piles, then, said Ken, I would know how many notes there were in the Mazatec speech scale.

Ken had also written of his use of a criterion word, or "frame" as he called it. The frame was a part of a sentence which was repeated over and over while new words were substituted one after another in the other part of the sentence. In this way, the pitch of the new word could be compared with the known pitch of the frame.

The first frame I used was "I bought a . . ."

It never worked well, for Catarina thoughtlessly shifted the tense. For several utterances she would say, "I bought a . . ."; then without warning the next utterance would be, "I'm going to buy a . . ." I got some results as long as I asked for words such as "oranges," "salt," "matches," "a horse," but when, following down my word list, I asked for the sentence, "I bought a flea," Catarina objected and refused to repeat such a silly thing.

I looked around for a frame that would take a wider variety of nouns, and chose a phrase which, literally, would be translated as "this here . . ." This time as I read down my word list, Catarina put "flea" through the frame without comment, and even such words as "nose" and "wife" were tested.

Marta sewed while she acted as informant, and with her mind on her sewing she repeated, without impatience or comment, anything we asked her. One time I thought I had been particularly boring. About two hundred times she had repeated a sentence, each time substituting a different noun for the subject. I had been listening to the repetitions, ready to record any variations in the tune of the sentence. I was tired, and I was sure that she must be. In the way of apology, and to show a bit of sympathy, I said, "I'm a big nuisance."

Marta, without a change of expression, and without looking up from her sewing, polly-parroted back, "I'm a big nuisance."

I hid my amusement and with no further comment went on working.

Florrie and I were trying to analyze the tone, but we were making very little progress. We were doubting our ability to come out with the answer when we received word that Ken was on his way to see us. The distance between us was considerable, especially if travel time was the measure. On his end of the road there was a three days' walk through the mountains, on our end of the road there was a one day's walk, and a half day's train ride lay in between. To him those five days of travel were a mere incident— he knew he could help us, and he was coming to do it.

On the twentieth of March, Ken arrived. Dehydrated from the long walk through territory without good water, he sat and drank tea while we besieged him with questions. The first hour or two it didn't matter much what he said—anything sounded good as long as it was said in English.

As soon as Ken's thirst for water and ours for English had been satisfied, he got down to the business of the day. He started explaining tone, and the ways and means of handling it. Lalo, his Mixtec informant, was traveling with him, and in order that we might see the technique in action, Ken put a list of words through various sentence frames. Lalo knew the procedure by this time, and the repetition of the sentences was all so easy for him that he sat and dozed, saying the words with his eyes closed and his chin resting on his chest. Every so often, to demonstrate to us that a wrong tone was startling enough to wake up the man, Ken used a tone which he himself knew to be wrong. Sleepily Lalo repeated the phrase after him; then hearing himself speaking incorrectly he came to with a shocked, "No! No!" He changed the phrase and immediately dozed off again until the next time Ken made a mistake.

The next day Ken, Florrie and I climbed the hill to Marta's hut and started our concentrated attack on Mazatec. With our informant, Marta, there were four of us sitting on wobbly chairs around an unpainted table. We listened, and this time our listening was guided by Ken as we compared this word with that word, this noun with that verb, this noun with that suffix. We listened several hours a day to words and more words, and the same words all over again.

Before Ken left two weeks later, the Lord had granted another of those petitions which he had requested that day under the pine tree. The technique which had given Ken his answer to the Mixtec problem had solved the Mazatec problem for Florrie and me. We now knew that the language had four essential pitches—high, semihigh, semilow, and low. The analysis still wasn't complete, however, for there were some tone glides at the end of words yet to be explained and which Ken felt to be important.

Now that we knew the number of essential pitches in the language, these pitches had to be written on the words which we had already collected for the dictionary as well as on all the words we had yet to collect. That task in itself seemed like an endless job of listening.

That day by day follow-up was a struggle. It took so much time for us to be sure that we had the correct tone written on a word, that sometimes we wondered if the tone were worth it. After all, the people understood us most of the time. Why bother with tone? Why not ignore it?

Then one evening when Silvia came over to visit, she picked up my notebook and started to read the Mazatec written there. When she read the sentence, *s'akoanna,* she pronounced the letters correctly, but she still looked puzzled. Then she looked up and inquired, "Does it say *s'akoanna* (speaking the second syllable with a low tone), or does it say *s'ako-anna*" (speaking that same syllable with a semilow tone)?

"What difference does it make?" I asked her, and she answered,

"One says that I learned just a little while ago, and the other says that I will learn soon now."

Then we knew beyond a doubt that the past was at times differentiated from the future by tone only. Immediately we thought of the New Testament and of the importance of such a distinction there. Specifically, in John 1:14 that same *koan* was used, and if it were said with a semilow tone the sentence would mean, "And the Word was made flesh"; whereas if it were said with a low tone the sentence would mean, "And the Word will be made flesh." There was I John 3:5: "Ye know that he was manifested to take away our sins." A similar change of the syllable *koan* and the verse would mean: "Ye know that he will be manifested to take away our sins."

We were convinced. We knew that the struggle must go on.

CHAPTER V

A Change of Location

(MAY — JULY, 1938)

WHEN WE FIRST CAME to Chalco, we had noticed that while a few of the people spoke Spanish, most of them spoke only Mazatec. It was not long before we became aware that the Mazatec-speaking people were considered inferior to those speaking Spanish. Those speaking Mazatec seemed to acknowledge the justice of such a judgment, and the ambitious ones struggled to better themselves by learning Spanish.

Florrie's and my work, for the most part, was to benefit the Mazatec speakers, and for that reason we wanted close association with them. We were finding, however, that it was hard to reach them because our house was on the main street and surrounded by those who spoke Spanish. That is, their efforts were in that direction; in a number of families the old generation spoke mostly Mazatec and some Spanish, the middle generation was bilingual, and the younger generation spoke more Spanish than Mazatec.

Our neighbors were merchants, the owners of shops which lined the streets, and as such were the intermediaries between the Mazatec people and the rest of Mexico. Of course, they had to know Spanish, for they dealt with the traveling salesmen and placed orders with firms in Tehuacán and Mexico City. They also had to know Mazatec, for the people of Chalco would not buy where only Spanish was spoken. The merchants knew that it was their knowledge of Spanish that made their shops profitable, and day by day they struggled to keep and to increase that knowledge. And it was a struggle, for they made up a Spanish island in the midst of a Mazatec sea.

These shopowners had welcomed Florrie and me as emissaries from the outside world who would help them in their fight for "civilized" culture. The eagerness with which they took us into the circle pleased and, at the same time, concerned us. One reason for our concern was that we tended to drift into their company instead of that of the Mazatec-speaking people. To chatter with them was the way of least resistance, for Spanish was easier for us than Mazatec. Of course, it was easier for Florrie because she had minored in it at the university, but even I found myself learning Spanish faster. I was learning it, in spite of the fact that all my study time was spent on Mazatec.

The very cordiality of the main-streeters troubled us, and their attentions and aspirations tired us, for their attitude made attendance at a funeral, wedding, or any other mixed gathering a feat needing delicate balance. It was only by trial and error that we learned that our best argument against marriage was that we'd make poor wives, for we neither knew how to grind corn nor to pat the dough into tortillas. That information usually brought them up short, for they believed their own adage that a Mazatec could no more work without tortillas than a donkey could work without corn. Not all men were convinced by that argument, however; some of them brushed it aside with the statement that they'd hire a maid to make the tortillas.

We determined to cultivate the friendship of the women and children and at the same time to show coolness toward the men. We hoped that if the people could see the contrast between the warmth with which we greeted and conversed with the women, and the reserve with which we conversed with the men, they would come to understand that we had a job to do, and that we had no intention of being sidetracked from it.

By watching Rufina and Silvia we picked up hints on Mazatec etiquette. We also noticed the manner with which they gave orders to men servants, and muleteers, and with which they greeted their social equals.

We went with them one evening to a school program. Some of the older pupils put on a skit, younger children sang songs, and others spoke pieces. For me the most outstanding thing of the program was the labored Spanish which the students spoke. It was apparent that for most of them Spanish was a foreign language, and it had taken considerable effort for them to learn their speeches.

The program was long, and it was almost midnight before it was finished. Because we had been sitting at the front, we were at the rear of the crowd as it was leaving. Our exit was a slow one, half a step at a time, but as we were making our way toward the door something seemed queer or different to me. I could not place it; I only knew that something about the crowd was definitely not American. The difference was not in the obvious—the straw hats, the embroidered costumes, the blanket coats—nor was it because language spoken by a crowd of Mazatecs had a different hum than language spoken by a crowd of Americans.

As we reached the door and stepped out into the square, I knew the answer. No car doors slammed; no cars were starting, backing, and idling. Instead, the characteristic noise was the scrape and clink of the men's hobnail sandals on dirt and stones. The crowd fanned out as the people took various paths home. We walked with those who went up the main street, and when we reached the cobblestone section, the clatter of the sandals increased—and more than ever I missed the purr and swish of an automobile.

Wheels did occasionally bump over the cobblestones, but they belonged to various wheelbarrows and one bicycle. The bicycle had been carried in from Tepetlán because there was no other way to get it over the trail. Even after it was in Chalco, only the main street, cut from the side of the mountain, was level enough for its use. In spite of the limited area in which it could be ridden, however, the bicycle was a triumph for Juan Sánchez who had bought it. He rode it up and down the street while twenty-five to thirty boys and men ran beside him, fascinated by its action.

Parades took the same route. National parades

with the band, dignitaries, soldiers, and school children marched so close to our door that we, standing on the sill, almost seemed to be part of the parade ourselves. Funerals, with the coffin balanced on the shoulders of four men, walked solemnly past. Wedding parties, in which everyone appeared happy but the bride, frequently went by on their way to the wedding feast.

Yes—the main street was an interesting place, but because we found ourselves spending more and more time with our Spanish-speaking neighbors, we felt that the translation would go ahead faster somewhere else. The time which we spent in casual conversation with our Spanish friends we felt to be lost. To us it seemed more advisable to chatter in Mazatec, but our neighbors—even the bilingual ones—refused to talk Mazatec with us. We sympathized with their attitude, knowing that they insisted on Spanish for one of the same reasons that we wanted to insist on Mazatec. They felt that they needed the practice in speaking Spanish, and they talked Mazatec only when relaxed, or when talking with someone who did not understand Spanish.

The only answer to the problem seemed to be for us to move to a place where our neighbors spoke only Mazatec, a place where we would rub elbows with a people who thought in Mazatec and whose gestures were a part of that language. Therefore, whenever we went for a walk, we were on a lookout for a vacant house. At first it seemed to us that there were a number of vacant houses, but when we inquired about this one or that one, we found that the owners who lived on their farms in the country came into town for market day or for fiestas. They didn't want to rent their houses because they used them on those days and considered them to be indispensable.

The house we were looking for could not be just any vacant house; it had to be surrounded by Mazatec-speaking neighbors and must be near someone who could be considered a fit chaperon for two single girls. We were also looking for a house with two rooms—most Mazatec houses had only one—and we thought we wanted adobe rather than the more usual thin board walls which left so many peek holes.

We found no place fulfilling those qualifications, but as we became more and more anxious to move away from that little Spanish clique on main street, we looked speculatively at Catarina's house. Although her house had only one room and seemed small, we agreed that we would be willing to live even in a house no better than that, if by doing so we could be in pure Mazatec surroundings.

We didn't ask Catarina for her house because it was obvious that she and her family were using it. Therefore, we were startled when she offered the house to us. Even as she was speaking, we remembered our conversation in which we agreed that we would be willing to live "in a house no better than Catarina's." Confident that the Lord directed even everyday events, we wondered if that might not be the house He intended us to have. He knew that we would not have considered it before, and had withheld Catarina's offer until we were willing to receive it.

The thought that the Lord was busying Himself about us personally was delightful, and reminded us that our real Protector remained the same in spite of a change of landlords. We had been a little concerned about exchanging a rich and powerful landlord for a poor and political nobody, but with the Lord directing, any such fear was unfounded.

In spite of the fascinating coincidence of Catarina's offer in relation to our state of mind, we didn't accept the house immediately. We considered it carefully with the original specifications in mind. The chaperon would be provided in Catarina herself. The Mazatec surroundings were good, for Marta, her brother Ramón, and her sister Eloísa, lived about thirty feet to the left. On the right side of the house, I could touch, at the same time, both the roof of the house which was offered us and the tiny kitchen house to which Catarina and her family were to move.

The neighbors behind and in front of the house were not as accessible, but it was not the distance that separated us. The incline of the mountain was the real separating feature, for due to it the floor of one neighbor's house was above Catarina's ridgepole, and the ridgepole of another neighbor's house was below Catarina's floor. We would have some contact with them, however, for the path from the center of town to the houses above went through our yard. When we ourselves went to the center, we would be passing through the midst of other homes, all Mazatec in speech and thought.

The walls of Catarina's house were of adobe, and even though the plaster had been knocked off in several places, they were still solid. Our objection to the house was that it was small and it had only one room. But we were willing to live in one room if by doing so we could hear Mazatec all our waking minutes. We told Catarina that we would move up if her husband would put a wooden floor over the dirt one, and build us a privy.

When the news got out that we intended to leave the main street, our merchant neighbors were horrified. Their reasoning and our private thoughts clashed at nearly every point. We were leaving a house with a tin roof, which to them signified wealth, and were moving into a house with a thatch roof. To them that was a step down on the social scale. (In reality, we preferred the thatch roof because the rain on the tin roof made so much noise that we had trouble hearing during our language lesson, while even a hard rain on the thatch roof did not disturb us.) To our merchant friends, to leave the main street was to leave the inner circle, the elite, the people of intelligence, and they did not believe that anyone would willingly, knowingly do so. They remonstrated with us. "Nobody lives up there." (Of course, by numerical count more people lived off the main street than on it.)

"It's so far!" (We were already three thousand miles from home. To us another quarter of a mile made no difference.)

"But it's so out of the center of things! Nothing goes on up there!" (Actually we'd be glad to get away. Drunks liked the center of activity too, and they often wandered to our door as they made their way up the main street. Watching the parades go by did not make up for that inconvenience.)

At first the Sánchez family refused to believe that we were leaving, and when at last they did believe it, they were hurt. They thought that we either did not like them, or did not like their house. Over and over we explained that we liked both them and their house, but that we needed to live among Mazatec-speaking people. Then, even without their understanding, we went ahead with our plans.

The man we hired to carry our goods for us selected a box of books and tied his carrying rope around it. Sitting on the floor, his back against the box, he took off his straw hat and slid the band of the carrying rope across the top of his head. Then he replaced his hat, barked a command at me, and while I steadied the box, he slowly stood up. Bent forward to balance the load, arms swinging in front of his knees, he walked up the hill. Florrie and I stood and watched him. With that load we had made the break; we had changed landlords. Rufina and Silvia watched him too—with tears in their eyes. We were glad they were still friends and hoped that later they would understand the necessity for our move.

When the man came back for another load, he brought two boys with him. One was Marcos, a ten-year-old adopted son of Catarina and Esteban. He was dressed in unpressed white muslin trousers and a dirty blue shirt. He stood leaning against the door without saying a word. The other boy was Tomás, Catarina's nephew. His father was a Spanish-speaking man from Tehuacán, and Tomás' heritage was reflected in the clothes he wore and in the fact that he could speak Spanish. Instead of white muslin trousers cut pajama style, his trousers were of heavier material cut American style. He greeted us shyly and then let us know that he wanted work, please. We hesitated about giving such a little fellow a load, but he would be disappointed if we didn't. We filled a waste basket with a few light things and handed it to him. His face shone with happiness and pride as he went out the door. Immediately the silent Marcos was beside us. Now that Tomás had been the spokesman, he was ready to carry, too.

All morning long we kept busy packing up loads, heavy ones for the man, little ones for Tomás, and middle-sized ones for Marcos. Florrie's trunk was too big for the man to carry by himself, and Esteban, Catarina's husband and our new landlord, was afraid to help him. He was afraid of the Sánchez family. He expected them to be angry at him for taking away their tenants. Because they were rich while he was poor, and they were politically powerful while he was a nobody, he didn't want them to know that he had anything to do with our moving. He waited until after dark and then dashed in with a friend, picked up the trunk, and hurried up the hill.

The next day the hired helper came back to finish his job, and by noon all our belongings were in a heap in the middle of Catarina's floor. The most important things to place and those which were given first consideration were our desks. Really they were only tables, but we spent many hours working

at them. In order to get good light, we put them
by the only window in the house. The window had
wooden shutters which we closed at night, but there
was no glass for the daytime and sometimes fog
smudged our papers. Our two army cots we put
in the corner beside a stack of wooden boxes which
made up our "dresser."

Our possessions would not all fit on one level in
that thirteen-by-twenty-foot house; so in order to
make use of a second level, we put planks across
some of the beams over our heads. We stored our
supplies there and climbed a ladder whenever we
needed them.

The end of the house which became the kitchen
had a two-burner kerosene stove, a table, a wash-
bowl, a tool chest, and more stacks of boxes for cupboards. Beside the only door stood two kerosene
cans holding our water supply for the day—about
eight gallons.

A few knickknacks, a few pictures here and there,
curtains covering the boxes, and the place became
home and once more we were ready for business.

CHAPTER VI

Translation Attempts

(AUGUST — SEPTEMBER, 1938)

LIVING IN A ONE-ROOM HOUSE wasn't too bad, but we lost our chance to study alone. Instead, we tried to concentrate with Tomás playing marbles on the floor, or with other children prodding us for explanations of the various pictures in our magazines. But at least hordes of school children no longer stopped by to watch us prepare and eat dinner.

Catarina's hens were a nuisance. They had considered that house to be home, and they did not give it up as easily as Catarina and her family did. With the door shut, they flew to the window sill and calmly looked for the next landing field—my bed, or Florrie's desk. I tried to discourage their entrance by throwing the nearest thing at hand in their direction. But I got tired of retrieving my eraser and pencils. I learned to keep a row of pebbles on my desk, for I could tosss one of them at a meditating hen with less interruption to my work.

Any inconvenience incurred by the exchange of a two-room house for a one-room house was more than made up for by the change which it caused in the attitude of the main street men. When they saw us leave the "rich" Sánchez home and voluntarily go to a people of lower class, they woke up to the fact that we were "different." They were puzzled and the pursuit relaxed—or perhaps pure inertia caused the change, for although they had always been ready to stop by for a look, they didn't bother to climb the hill. Whatever the reason for the change, the relief was wonderful.

Florrie and I were more satisfied, too, when we could see ourselves making progress in language learning. With our neighbors on the hill we were not tempted to talk Spanish, and even when our Mazatec was jumbled, they tried to figure out what we had said. They applauded our stumbling words, appreciative of the fact that we wanted to talk with them.

Every time Florrie and I learned a new word, we wrote it on a three-by-five inch slip of paper and put it in a file box. For each of the Mazatec words in my file box I wrote an English translation, whereas Florrie translated hers into Spanish. These slips alphabetized became our dictionaries, and as our knowledge grew, our dictionaries increased in size. We filed prefixes and suffixes and parts of words too, and in this way our boxes were not only dictionaries but baby grammars as well. We studied vocabulary by memorizing our dictionaries, and because of frequent review we learned new words without forgetting too many of the old ones.

Frequently we'd come to recognize a Mazatec word and understand what the people were talking about, but still not be sure of its English or Spanish equivalent. Sometimes Marta could make us understand its meaning by describing the situation in which the word was used, or by making up sentences which used it in various ways. Catarina, on the other hand, was not as intelligent as Marta, and her answers were often frustrating. For example, in all the situations in which I had heard the words *nt'ia* and *ni'ya,* both could have meant "house." Following the theory that no two words had exactly the same meaning, I tried to find out the difference between them. I asked Catarina, "When do you say *nt'ia* and when do you say *ni'ya?*"

She answered, "We say both words any day we want to say them. We don't have special days for saying one and special days for saying the other."

I tried again. "When do you use the word *ni'ya?*"

"We use it when we are talking, of course!" Then because she was disgusted at my silly questions, I changed the subject. Not until two or three years later did I decide that *nt'ia* meant "house" whereas *ni'ya* meant "home."

At times we learned the meaning of a sentence by watching the reaction of the person to whom we said it. But, when doubtful of our information, we didn't like to try it out on just anybody, so we usually tried it first on Catarina or Marta. One day because I was in doubt of a certain phrase, I asked Catarina, "Is it all right if I say ' . . . '?"

"Yes," she answered, but she didn't look very convinced, so I asked again, "Is it all right if I say it that way?"

"Yes, you may if you want to." Then after a long pause she added, "But no one will understand you."

Catarina was not the only one who tried my patience. Inés, a fifteen-year-old girl who lived next door, loved to tease, and a language lesson provided the opportunity. She mimicked Catarina's teaching and mimicked our replies, and if we still succeeded in ignoring her, she grabbed our pencils. Catarina tried to send her home but without success, and not until Inés herself became bored did she go.

Even without Inés' teasing I found language study tedious. We spent hours looking for ways of expressing the future, the past tense, and the direct objects. Some constructions were especially difficult because only the tone indicated which was which. Typical were the sentences: "I am giving it to you," "I am giving it to him," and "He is giving it to him." They were alike but for the pitch with which they were said.

By dint of much effort, I was learning to distinguish the different tones as I heard them in conversation, but frequently I missed and sometimes with startling results. There was the time I was helping a girl to memorize Bible verses. She was having a hard time, and it embarrassed her when a child happened in and heard her stumbling efforts. "Go away! Go away!" she said to the little girl. "Don't stay around here. This is a holy thing."

Her statement surprised me, but I hoped that it was an indication that she was coming to appreciate the Scriptures. The child went away but almost immediately she was back again.

"Go away!" the girl insisted. "This is . . ."

The tone of that last phrase shocked me. The letters were the same as for a "a holy thing," but if I had heard the tone correctly this time she had said,

"Go away! Don't stay around here. This is dumb stuff!"

Which of those two times did my ears catch the true pitch? I never knew, and consequently I never knew what she had actually said. If it had been one of our regular informants who had confused me, I could have asked her to repeat, for they had learned that tone was hard for us, and they were accustomed to repeating. This girl, however, would only have been embarrassed that we had picked up her remark.

Marta seldom tired of repeating, and she especially enjoyed helping us to translate Bible stories. Her eyes shone as she saw each story develop. Eloísa, her sister, liked them too, and she listened while sewing or cooking nearby, and added her suggestions whenever Marta hesitated. Although only sixteen years old, Eloísa herself developed into a very able informant, and when Marta was busy she frequently took over.

On one of those days I was working with some of the more common salvation verses, among them John 14:6: "Jesus saith unto him, I am the way, the truth, and the life: no man cometh unto the Father, but by me." The Spanish phrase, "but by me," meant nothing to Eloísa, and in order to explain it to her, I put a book in the center of the table. "Suppose that this is God," I told her, speaking in Mazatec. "Suppose that this is the road that leads to God," and I laid my pencil in position. "We use a road to go from Chalco to Tepetlán, and also we use a road to go from earth to Heaven. Jesus said that He is the road. People may try to reach God some other way, but Jesus said, 'No man can come to God "but by me" [those three words said in Spanish] for I am the road.' " Eloísa had been watching and listening intently; now thoughtfully she supplied the missing Mazatec phrase for "but by me." (Florrie had long before noticed that there was a vital connection between my appetite and the results of my language lesson. That little phrase, "but by me," made my dinner taste good that day.)

A few days later, working with Marta on John 3:16, I wanted to get the phrase, "should not perish," or as it was translated in the Spanish, "should not be lost." Sometimes when lacking a word I would tell a story, building up to an obvious conclusion but stopping before I reached it. As Marta continued the story I would listen, hoping that she would use the missing word. Accordingly, in order to learn how to say that a person was lost, I started a story. "One day you wanted to go from Chalco to Tepetlán, but you went down the wrong trail. You walked and walked but didn't find the right trail. After a long time you stopped. You didn't know where Chalco was. You didn't know where Tepetlán was. You didn't know where any of the other villages were. You didn't know where to go, and you said. . . . What did you say?"

Marta thought a bit, and then continued the story with, "I don't know where the trail is."

Eyes on my face, she saw that I was not satisfied, so she changed to, "I can't see the trail."

I tried again with another story. "Your little niece Rosa left the house one afternoon and she didn't come back. You looked for her and didn't find her. It got dark, and still she didn't come back. You didn't know where Rosa was. What did you say? You said, 'Rosa is . . .' "

Marta finished with, "Rosa is sleeping some place else."

That answer discouraged both of us, but although I left that phrase for a while and went on to something else, nevertheless I kept it in mind as something to be on the alert for.

A couple of weeks later while I was working with Catarina, she picked up my fountain pen. Perhaps because she could neither read nor write fountain pens fascinated her, and she was delighted when as she slowly pulled the pen across her hand it left a trail of ink behind. For a little relief from the boring job of recording verb conjugations, I took the pen from her and wrote on her hand, spelling out her name as I did it, "C-a-t-a-r-i-n-a."

"There now," I told her in broken Mazatec, "if you are lacking yourself, here is your name."

Catarina chuckled, and corrected my sentence, "Now if I am lost, here is my name."

The sound of, "I am lost," made me jump, and Catarina chuckled again, happy that she had pleased me even though she didn't know how.

But Florrie and I had other troubles with John 3:16, for the phrase, "everlasting life," still perplexed us. "Life" was not something we could touch while we asked, "What is this?" and our descriptions had brought no results. Using Spanish, we had asked our bilingual friends, and they had given us the word which was also used for "heart." That was a possibility, and we wondered if in Mazatec the word for "heart" and "life" were the same.

With some misgivings we started through the First Epistle of John using the word "heart" for "life." A few verses went smoothly, but others were impossible with no more knowledge than we had at the time. First John 3:14 did not seem too bad: "We know that we have passed from death unto life, because we love the brethren," but, perhaps because we were still uneasy about the word "life," we read our translation to Catarina and asked her to tell us in Spanish what we had said.

She sat thoughtful for a minute after we had finished reading, and then said, "We know that when we passed by, we died of heart disease."

She had added the word "disease," perhaps because she had been trying to make sense out of something that she did not understand. In spite of its inaccuracy, her translation had shown us that the word "heart" was not an equivalent of the word "life." But what was the word? Somewhere, somehow, we must find it.

We had a chance for a different approach to the problem when Alberto, a ten-year-old neighbor boy, was dying of pneumonia. With no periodical in town, all news was carried by the grapevine and we put our ear to it and listened for the word "life." When we saw a friend come up the hill from Alberto's house, we called out and asked, "How's Alberto?"

"He's serious," our friend answered. "He stopped eating several days ago. Today he no longer talks." (The Mazatec people judged a person's condition by means of certain recognized symptoms. Usually loss of appetite was the first to denote a serious illness. When the patient no longer talked, the second symptom, his case was considered very serious indeed. At the third, cold feet, friends and relatives gathered to sit with the family and wait for death. Of course, the length of time between those symptoms varied from patient to patient, and how much it varied and the subsidiary steps in between—crazy talk, bubbling throat and the like—were always the subject of much discussion.)

We added a different note when we asked, "Is he living?" (We knew the verb "to live"; it was the noun "life" which we were lacking.)

"Yes, he is living."

"What is it that makes you say he is living? What is it that he has now that a dead person doesn't have?" Our friend looked puzzled and did not know how to answer. Another friend went by, and again we asked questions but without success. Our next news was that the boy's feet were cold, and a day or so later he died.

"He's dead?"

"Yes."

"What does he have?"

"He has death."

"What did he have before?"

"I don't know."

The grapevine had failed. We still didn't know the word for "life."

Next we tried our old friends, the Sánchez family. Of all the people we knew, they spoke the two languages, Spanish and Mazatec, best. We had asked them before, but perhaps if we asked again for the Mazatec equivalent of the Spanish word "life" they would think of it this time. We stood in the store and after a little polite chatter we reached the point of our visit. "How do you say in Mazatec 'has everlasting life'?"

Rufina, Silvia, and their mother talked among themselves, first in Spanish, then in Mazatec, and back to Spanish again as they tried out one phrase after another. With none of them were they satisfied, and so they gave us the advice we had often received and which we were to receive many times more, "Ask some old man who knows both languages well. Only someone like that will be able to tell you these things."

The advice was good and so we thanked them for it, knowing as we did so that neither they nor anyone else had been able to tell us who such a man might be.

Paulina, Mrs. Sánchez' older sister, was in the store at the time. Unlike Mrs. Sánchez, who wore shoes and American-style dresses, Paulina was still barefoot and in the Mazatec costume. Now, after her influential sister and educated nieces had given up, Paulina mumbled shyly into her shawl, "We wouldn't say 'has everlasting life.' We would say, 'shall never have death.'"

That was the best we could do. Florrie worked through the Gospel of John writing "not death" whenever she came to the word "life," and sometimes it took considerable thought before she could bring out the sense of the verse that way. John 10:10 was the trickiest: "I am come that they might have life, and that they might have it more abundantly." The best she could do with that was, "I am come that they might not have death, not even a little bit."

In this way Florence worked at the Gospels, and a year or two later she continued with the Epistles with Enedina, a married sister of Marta's. They watched the Spanish, but because Enedina knew so little of it, Florrie helped her by explaining each verse as best she could in Mazatec. After a while Florrie no longer had to explain the Spanish word "life," for Enedina had learned that in such a place Florrie expected "not death."

Then one day Enedina did not say "not death"— she said *kjoavijnachon* instead. Florrie corrected her, and they passed on. A few days later they came to the word "life" again, and again instead of saying "not death" Enedina said *kjoavijnachon*. That time, however, she objected to Florrie's correction with, "*Kjoavijnachon* means that which is not death."

Could it be that we had found the word "life" at last! We checked with monolinguals, "Do dead people have *kjoavijnachon?*"

"No."

"Do people who are living all have *kjoavijnachon?*"

"Yes."

We checked with the Sánchez family. "What does *kjoavijnachon* mean in Spanish?"

They looked thoughtful, and then almost shouted, "Why, that is the word for 'life'! Who told you?"

They were as delighted as we were to know the Mazatec equivalent. They had tried to think of it, but it is frequently difficult to translate from one language to another. Perhaps they could have remembered, if they had first thought of a situation in which the Spanish word "life" was used, and then had talked about the situation in Mazatec. The best bilingual informant does not merely give Spanish words versus Mazatec words; rather, he thinks of a situation and tells what is said in both languages for that one situation.

That was in 1940 that we finally found the word for "life." Back in 1938 we still talked with difficulty, and only the most common phrases came without effort. Our purpose in coming to Mexico, however, was ever before us, and already we were telling our closest neighbors and most frequent visitors any of the Bible truths which we knew how to express.

One of our frequent visitors was Ida, a relative of Marta and sister of Rosa. She studied verses with us, but she also liked to play with the jumping jacks that Florrie had brought from the States, and she spent hours looking at old copies of the *National Geographic*.

One morning when she slipped in at breakfast time, neither the jumping jacks nor the magazines interested her. She waited quietly until we had finished eating, then told us that her mother had sent her to ask for a bit of cotton. We had been asked for old pieces of carbon paper with which to copy a new embroidery pattern, for pencil and help in writing a letter, for other small favors, but this was the first time we had ever been asked for cotton. As I got it for her I asked, "How will your mother use it?"

"Nina is very sick. She will probably die." That expression, "she will probably die," came so easily to the people there that I was not too concerned, but I inquired Mazatec fashion about her welfare. No, she was not eating; she had stopped two days ago. No, she was not talking. She had fever. Her head was very hot while, yes, her feet were very cold. Then the significance of the cotton struck me.

The law of the region demanded that a person be buried within twenty-four hours, and a funeral was so involved that the family frequently started preparations ahead of time. Because no ready-made coffins were for sale, the sick person was measured and the order given to the local carpenter. Dinner must be served to the mourners, and to fulfill this need hens or turkeys were frequently bought in advance and kept alive at the house ready for use.

It was Mazatec custom to straighten out a dead person, lay his arms across his chest, close his eyes, but they did not close his mouth. The mouth, which usually fell open during the final period of weakness, stayed as it was, and a little bit of cotton was stuffed in the opening. As part of the preparation for Nina's funeral, Ida had been sent for cotton.

Nina was Ida's and Rosa's older sister. Because she was older, she had duties at home which kept her from being the frequent visitor that Ida was, but I felt her to be a friend. That she was that near death came as a shock, and even as I handed the cotton to Ida the question came to me, "Has she been told that through Christ she could have eternal life, and only through Him?"

Nina spoke no Spanish and would not have understood if told in that language. As far as I knew, there was not one Mazatec-speaking person who would have told her, for there were none who believed that message themselves. For that same reason no Spanish-Mazatec speaker would have told her. Probably only two people both knew Mazatec and believed the Gospel. One of those was Florrie and the other was I; and, even though our speaking ability was still in the stutter-and-guess stage, that put the responsibility right on our doorstep.

Quickly I ran over in my mind all the occasions on which I had seen Nina. Had I ever told her that Jesus did not stay dead when He died on the cross but that He was alive again and in Heaven? Had I ever told her that Christ was the road to Heaven and only because of Him could she hope to arrive? Had I ever told her that Christ loved her even though she was a sinner? I didn't know how to tell her much, but I could have managed that much. But I didn't remember that I had.

Perhaps Florrie had. I asked her. No, she couldn't remember that she had either. Then I felt like a slacker. Christ had provided the means whereby Nina and all sinners could be pardoned. He had taken upon Himself her sentence. If she put her confidence in Him, her life in the next world would be all joy. But how could she put her confidence in

Him—she didn't know Him, and I had not told her about Him.

I was ashamed. What kind of servant was I? So I prayed. I prayed the Lord not to let her die yet, even though the carpenter was making her coffin; and I prayed that somehow I'd have a chance to tell her the things I should have told her before.

Late that afternoon I saw Ida coming up the path and could hardly wait for her to get inside the house before asking, "How's Nina?"

"She's talking again," Ida told me. Her mother had sent her to ask me to come and take her temperature. I said I would, and as I looked for the thermometer and got out alcohol and cotton, I thanked the Lord for the excuse to go. Ida and I walked down the path together, and as we went I was glad that because she was a child I would be excused from conversation. I was concentrating so hard trying to remember Bible verses and Mazatec words that I couldn't think up small talk at the same time.

I was taken directly to the spot where Nina lay on a straw mat in the center of the floor. A burlap bag was her only blanket, and Rosa's lap was a pillow. There the taking of a temperature was more ceremonial than diagnostic. None of her family could read a thermometer or interpret the information when it was read to them. They knew that the educated and the rich took a sick person's temperature, and they wanted the best for Nina.

I was no sooner seated on the mat beside Nina than we were completely surrounded by interested relatives. I didn't pay much attention to them. I was too busy sizing up Nina's condition. She responded when I spoke to her, and seemed to understand.

I put my thermometer under her arm, and as I held it there I told her what I could about Christ. Then, because the verses we had been working on were probably more accurate than sentences I could make up at the moment, and because the Word of God is living and powerful, I started to teach her John 3:16. As I said it to her phrase by phrase, not only Nina repeated it but the guests chimed in too, and by the time the thermometer had registered they had memorized it. Nina seemed to understand, and as I thought that perhaps she believed I felt tremendous relief. I wanted to help her medically, but her condition puzzled me, and I didn't know how.

As I climbed the path home I relaxed. For the moment the job was done, and I hoped that in the future I'd not be caught short that way again. I intended to see to it that my friends were told before their feet got cold.

Nina didn't die the next day, nor the day after that. In fact, the event had been put off indefinitely. That embarrassed and annoyed her family. What should they do with the unused coffin? Surely people with good judgment would not have ordered it built! I couldn't exactly apologize for their embarrassment, even though it may have been the Lord's answer to my plea that had upset their calculations, so I gave them a picture book instead. With some pictures to look at and something other than Nina to talk about they felt better, and I did too.

CHAPTER VII

One "R"

EVEN AS WE STRUGGLED to increase our vocabulary and to fathom the intricacies of Mazatec grammar, we were conscious of the fact that were the translation of the New Testament complete, perfect, and printed, a tremendous task would still remain ahead of us. Certainly not more than one Mazatec out of twenty could read with any degree of understanding, and not until the other nineteen had mastered the printed page could they receive full value from the Bible.

Neither Florrie nor I had been trained as teachers, but we were finding that if as Bible translators we did not become teachers, much of our labors would be valueless. In fact, to be teachers was not enough: we must become authors of primers and reading helps as well.

We had one advantage over United States educators, for only with considerable memory drill could they teach the English pupil to read such words as "bee," "tea," "we," "key," "ski," and "rough," "though," and "cough." Our advantage lay in the fact that we ourselves had prepared the alphabet and primers for a previously unwritten language. Consequently, the Mazatec materials were phonetically written; that is, there was a one-for-one correspondence between symbol and sound unit. Once the student had learned the value of the various letters, he could read new words with less drill than that required by an English student.

In other respects we were at a disadvantage. In the United States, literacy was the common thing. Children saw and handled books as soon as they could toddle, and they grew up expecting to read them. The Mazatecs, on the other hand, considered that only the exceptional person would learn, and few of them expected to be among that number. This attitude set up a mental barrier which we found difficult to overcome.

Spanish was the language of the educated, and of the state and federal government. It was the language used in court and the language in which deeds to property were written. Perhaps because of this situation and because there had been no literature in the Mazatec language, the Mazatecs held their own language in contempt. With the same adjective with which they described a cripple, an idiot, and a person wanting in money or goods, they also described their own language, and "word" plus that adjective made up a compound word meaning, "Indian language." The people had to be convinced that their language was worthy of being written, that it was possible to write it, and that it would profit them to read and write it.

Men, literate or illiterate, plan for the disposal of their property after death. The literate man, if he so chooses, makes a will while he is strong and while his mind is vigorous. When he is sick, he is not troubled with such affairs and his actual departure is undisturbed by such details.

In contrast to this, the death of an illiterate Mazatec may be a harrowing affair. Unless he has had his wishes recorded by the court secretary, his "will" is made orally and perhaps under trying circumstances. According to custom, when he feels himself to be seriously ill, he gathers together his family and tells them his wishes. The news of his illness spreads, however, and hopeful as well as loving relatives flock to his side. Many weep as they discuss his imminent death, and many a weeping one, as she clings to his arm, begs, "What are you leaving me, Godfather?"

Because it is his spoken word which disposes of the property, everyone wants to hear what his last spoken word will be. Relatives bring their blankets and sleep on the floor in the same room with the dying man. Of course, many come in true friendship, but hope of gain is frequent.

After the death, if the listening family or the relatives do not agree as to what the dead man said, or if one brother wants more than his father said he was to have, a quarrel may split the family, and one or more of its members may be murdered. In this way many violent deaths can be traced to illiteracy.

Some parents make a special effort to have at least one of their children go to school. The occasional family succeeds in sending a boy to the city for his education, but they have no way of communicating with him while he is gone. If the son writes to them, they turn his letter round and round, but, until they find someone who can read it to them, they can only wonder what emergency caused him to write.

While Florrie's and my purpose in studying Mazatec was to give the people the Bible, nevertheless we were conscious of the benefits which the Mazatec people would receive if their society should change from an illiterate to a literate one, and we hoped that along with the Bible they would receive these benefits.

Mr. Townsend, the director of our group of Bible translators, had taught some of the Cakchiquel Indians of Guatemala to read, and at the Summer Institute of Linguistics he had passed on to us some of the principles of primer construction. He recommended controlling the vocabulary used in the primers, and thereby starting the lessons with only three or four letters of the alphabet. The other letters were to be added gradually as the lessons progressed.

When we tried to make a primer for the Mazatec, we found the process was made more complicated because of tone. How was it to be taught when each word had to be said on some specific pitch? We decided that we would start to teach tone in the first lesson. We chose to begin with the words "my mother" and "our mother," because they were spelled simply and were alike but for one of the marks indicating tone. That mark was all that distinguished the "my" from "our."

Catarina was one of our first pupils. She knew that the words, "my mother" and "our mother," looked almost alike; and without bothering to think, she said whichever word came into her head. I tried to make her conscious of the tone marks by telling her that she sang when she talked, and I backed up my argument by humming the pitch of the two words. Her response was a look of disbelief—certainly she should know when she was singing and when she was not!

Not only the tone, but the alphabet itself was a problem. To us it seemed preferable to have letters as nearly like the Spanish as possible. When this alphabet was used, those who already read Spanish transferred that learning to Mazatec with a minimum of effort. And those who were not accomplished readers, but had been to school a year or two, put to use any knowledge they had.

We tried the alphabet, not only with beginning students, but with more advanced readers also. Our first extensive experiment was done with Eloísa. She had reached the third grade in school and was able to read Spanish fairly well. We watched while she read Mazatec, making note of the letters which were the hardest for her, and if we were able, we exchanged them for letters which she read more easily. Then we typed out the Bible stories which we had translated into Mazatec and gave them to her. At first she needed help in reading them, but she enjoyed them so much that she practiced until she could read them by herself.

Rita, a married sister, had been to school too; and when she came to call, Eloísa slid the sheets under her nose and stood by, teasing, laughing, helping, until Rita, too, had read the story. Florrie and I were encouraged by Eloísa's enthusiasm, for we knew that we could not personally teach each of fifty thousand people. We knew that if the Mazatecs were to learn, they must help each other, and in Eloísa we had the first evidence that some at least would be willing to do so.

Florrie and I found ourselves counting more and more on sixteen-year-old Eloísa. Quick and intelligent, with ability to read, she made a better informant than her sister Marta. Because of her captivating ways, other people followed her lead, and we hoped that Rita was just one of many whom she would persuade to read the Bible.

While we were leaning on that hope, we were told that she was to be married. The news shouldn't have surprised us for she was charming, and sixteen was marrying age among the Mazatecs. We started to console ourselves with the thought that she could work with us even after her marriage, but that hope too was dashed—the man she was marrying was from Rio Seco, a town eight hours away. Of course, we took time off from our studying to go to the wedding. We wanted to see who was the fortunate man getting our Eloísa.

We had known that the match had been arranged, for proper Mazatec matches were, but I was surprised when at the bride's house somebody poked me in the ribs from the right at the same time I was jabbed with an elbow from the left. In both ears I heard the hiss, "She's the one who arranged it." I looked in the direction the jabs seemed to indicate and saw a stately, pleasant-looking woman. Then someone repeated the statement out loud and the woman acknowledged it with a dignified bow. Head held high, she recognized that she was an important figure at the festival. And she was. Eloísa was an orphan and if she was to make a respectable marriage, some adult relative had to take the responsibility.

A Mazatec wedding consists of several parts. The first is the civil marriage. The second is a ceremonial head washing of the bride and groom. The third is optional, an all-night dance at the home of the bride. The fourth is marriage by the priest. The fifth is a banquet and dance at the home of the groom. The sixth is a dinner in honor of the wedding godparents. Each of these parts takes its full quota of time, and frequently the wedding festival covers most of three days.

On the second day, after Eloísa's head had been washed, the wedding party passed on to complete the ceremony at the home of the groom. Florrie and I did not go with them, for we preferred to stay with Eloísa. The house which a minute before had been overrun with guests became empty, and Florrie and I found ourselves alone with her. Just for a little small talk Florrie asked, "What is your husband's name?"

She tried to smile, but tears trickled down her face as she sobbed, "I don't know."

Eloísa's tears disturbed us, and we asked Rita about them. Rita was immediately on the defensive, "We told her to cry!"

"Why?"

"Because if she doesn't cry, everybody will think she was the one who wanted the marriage arranged."

We remembered the wedding parties we had seen pass, all with tearful brides. Could it be that they looked sad purposely? Perhaps, but Eloísa's tears had seemed genuine to us and they had every reason to be. She was leaving home to go to a family which she hardly knew, and to a town she had visited only once or twice. She would live in the house in which her husband had been raised and would become a servant to her mother-in-law. Of course, she was not considered a servant; it was just that she needed to be trained to make her husband's coffee and to cook his meals the way he had been accustomed to have them. And because she was still young the relatives would check to be sure she washed his clothes clean.

Eloísa may have been reminded that it was customary to weep, but certainly she needed no urging. She walked in her procession as the other brides had done, eyes downcast, her face stiff with face powder caked by the tears.

At the banquet the bride and groom were put at the head of the table, and not until then did I get a good look at the groom. He was probably a year or so older than Eloísa, clean, with a good face and build. As I watched them, I began to feel sorry for the fellow. After all Eloísa was his wife, and he was trying to be nice to her, but she wouldn't even look at him, and when he spoke to her she wouldn't answer. Custom demanded that the bride and groom eat from the same plate, but even so Eloísa managed to keep her back to her husband. An arranged marriage had not done away with the necessity for courting; the groom was trying as hard as any suitor ever did. Apparently he was successful, for when they came to call on us a week later, their eyes were like stars and neither one could keep his eyes off the other.

After Eloísa had gone with her husband to Rio Seco, Florrie and I settled down to business again. Our beginning pupils had discouraged us about our primer. Catarina was not the only one who had difficulty reading words distinguished by tone. We threw that first attempt aside and made up an entirely different primer. In the new one we didn't contrast the various tones; instead for the first ten pages we used only those words which were spoken on the next to the lowest tone. It placed a considerable limitation on the permitted vocabulary, but we wanted the pupils to have a good start on the letters in the alphabet before confusing them with tone.

Then, the new primer in hand, we offered to teach Inés to read. She had never been to school, and, like most of the Mazatec adults, felt that she was too stupid to learn. Habitually her answer to our offer was, "I can't learn; my head is hard."

Then one day I didn't ask Inés. I told her, "Sit down and I'll teach you to read." She giggled, said she couldn't, but sat. We had anticipated that "can't" complex, and in order to overcome it we had made the first lesson very simple.

"There, Inés, look. That word says 'boy.' "

"Boy," she repeated.

"And this one says 'children.' "

"Children."

"All right; now what does this one say?"

"Boy."

"That's right, Inés! And you said you couldn't read!"

So we went on to another word and then came back to "boy" and "children." After a bit, Inés, out of breath and hands atremble, was able to point to each one correctly. The first lesson was over, and she promised to come back for another.

As she went out the door she met Catarina. Perhaps her head was carried a trifle higher than usual. Anyway something made Catarina ask, "What were you doing in there?"

"Reading," Inés answered.

Once started, Inés needed no urging. Every day she came back, and although she didn't ask for a lesson, she stood around hopefully until we remembered why she had come. She no longer bothered us at our language lessons with Catarina, for her attitude changed completely. She still loved to tease and talk, but while we were studying she was quiet. She even tried to help us, correcting some of the more atrocious errors in our speech. When we asked her, she'd explain the meaning of a word for us, but her patience gave out if we didn't catch on quickly.

We hadn't planned to teach children, for they could go to the government school. Even though the lessons were taught in Spanish there they would eventually learn something. We intended to spend our time with adults who were beyond school age, but Tomás, though barely six, wormed his way past our objections. At least twice a day he came in with, "I want to read." At the end of a ten- or fifteen-minute lesson he wanted to be off again, but at that he outdistanced Catarina. (She tried, but we never did have much success with her.) Perhaps it was Tomás' enthusiasm which carried him along. Frequently he appeared before breakfast and wiggled with impatience when we told him to come back later. Neither did he have sympathy with Sunday as a "day of rest," for he wanted to study on those days, too. One Sunday he was in four times asking for a lesson. The last time was 9:30 P.M., and his parting words as he ran off to bed were, "You will teach me tomorrow, won't you?"

When, a few days later, Florrie brought out a paint book and crayons and showed Tomás how to use them, he knew complete satisfaction. After coloring the first picture he stopped long enough to turn the pages and tell us, "Look at all the work I have to do." All afternoon he colored, but toward evening he came to me in my professional character as nurse. "My finger hurts," he told me. There was a blister at the site of the rubbing pencil.

I put a bandage on it and then asked, "Don't you think you had better rest a little?"

"Yes," he said, but promptly went back to his coloring, working as hard as ever.

He was around the house so much that we gave him a pencil and started him writing. He liked to do it and practiced his letters quite contentedly. "Look," he said one day as he drew a wiggly line for an *s*, "this is a good *s*; it's only a little bit ugly."

Marcos, our landlord's adopted son, caught the spirit and wanted to learn. Because he was already doing a man's job, he was not free to study in the daytime, and he was so tired he wanted to be in bed by 7:30. He returned from work sometime between five and six, ate his second meal of the day, and came right over. Usually when he arrived we were eating. A few times we refused to be interrupted, but more often our consciences made us help him—it was his only chance and he wanted very much to learn. Frequently I ate my supper with my fork in my right hand and a pointer in the left. Both of us tried, Marcos concentrating on the lesson and I on ways of teaching him, but we didn't get on very well. Compared to little Tomás, he seemed impossibly slow. Finally I stopped teaching him from the primer and helped him to memorize Bible verses instead. I knew that they would do him good, and I saw no evidence that he would be able to read for himself very soon.

By the end of September, Florrie and I were more competent to judge the primer and its qualities. We knew some of its weak points and parts needing revision. Of our five pupils, Marta liked to read if we were with her but did not push ahead by herself; reading was play for Tomás and he enjoyed it as he enjoyed coloring; Catarina and Marcos were slow and uncertain; Inés was our shining star—persistent, determined, no fiesta was important enough to keep her from a lesson.

One day after Inés had finished the primer, I typed out John 14:6 and gave it to her to read. I don't know who was more thrilled, she or I, when she spelled it through. She went over it again and again until she could read it smoothly. "Take it home," I told her, "and read it to your brother and grandmother."

"Oh, yes," she answered excitedly.

The next day she was back, the slip on which the verse was written now protected by a larger piece of paper. She wanted another verse, so that day we gave her John 3:16, and the next day Romans 10:9, 10. Those little slips of paper meant a lot to Florrie and me. We didn't see them as pieces of paper with Mazatec words on them; to us they were "Scripture in circulation"—the first Mazatec Scripture ever to be circulated.

CHAPTER VIII

Etiquette

(OCTOBER, 1938 — MARCH, 1939)

THE MOUNTAINS which made up the view south of our house were beautiful, and we sometimes counted the ranges visible. On some foggy days we could not see even one range. Rainy days we might see two. On clear days we could see up to five. If we could have parachuted into our yard, probably we would have considered the mountains to the west as beautiful as we considered those to the south, but because we had come in by horseback, we could not disassociate the feel of them from the way they looked.

Clouds against the southern ranges looked cool and pleasant; we had ridden the western ones and knew them to be blistering in the sun and chilling in the rain. In our lack of knowledge we could imagine the southern ranges to be close together, with the trail dipping just out of sight; we knew that between the western ranges were knee-tiring downs and breath-consuming ups. The southern ranges made a picture framed by our doorway; the western ones were obstacles shutting us in and isolating us from the rest of the world.

In distance we were not far from Mexico City

(about 250 miles); we could have come and gone easily but for the mountains. Sometimes they seemed oppressive, for we could not leave Chalco without crossing them. We knew that we could never leave on short notice, for each trip required riding animals, pack animals, and a guide. The muleteers knew our helplessness and charged exorbitant prices, and even after arrangements had been made with one, the owner might change the day of his departure, or arrive at the house without enough animals for the baggage. Because the arrangements were so trying we felt a sense of relief when we pulled away from the door even though we knew the day would be a difficult one.

It had been nine months since we had been in Mexico City, and the thought of meeting our American friends delighted us. The first hour or two on the trail was pleasant, for as we rode we could watch the sunrise, hear the birds wake up, and then see the fog lift from the valleys. But the hours dragged on, and as we started down the other side of the highest mountain the moss-covered trees changed to thorny shrubs. The horses' feet no longer splashed us with mud; instead they kicked up dust that settled in layers on our boots and riding skirts. At San Fernando the trail dropped rapidly to the river and only a series of switchbacks kept the road at an incline practical for riding and pack animals.

Perhaps because of losing altitude so quickly, I became mountain sick. Perhaps the hot sun was affecting me—something made me nauseated and dizzy. Perhaps my trouble came from the cloud of dust stirred up by approaching and passing mule teams. The muleteers had a preferred schedule; three days a week they left Tepetlán for Chalco, and three days a week they came back. It so happened that we were traveling down to Tepetlán at the same time many of them were traveling up. We must have met fifty different animals that day just in that part of the trail. If I could stick it out until we were beyond the switchbacks I was sure I'd feel better. Maybe if I kept yawning I wouldn't lose the bit I had eaten but it is unpleasant to yawn with the air full of dust and the smell of sweating mules. I thought as we turned the last sharp corner that I had won, but just as my head told me that I should be better, the world began to dance. I staggered from my horse and dropped beside the trail. We had come to a pocket, the spot where two ranges met, and the atmosphere seemed stifling, too thick to breathe.

The mountain rose sharply from the trail on the left, and although the slope off to the right was more gradual, even it provided no place for resting. To lie that close to a busy trail was dangerous, and Florrie and our landlord-guide, Esteban, were conscious of that fact. Nothing concerned me, however—I didn't even have the energy to lift my head when vomiting.

As I began to feel better I became embarrassed. What would I look like to passing muleteers! And I felt sorry for Florrie. How concerned she was—but probably it was the biting red ants that actually got me on my way again. Clinging to the saddle horn, leaning far forward with my head almost on the horse's neck, I traveled with my eyes closed while Esteban led the horse.

We went slowly, quietly, until a ledge crossed the trail. Then Esteban would say, "Open your eyes." I'd open them and sit up until past the difficult spot, and then close them again. How patient Esteban was! I was grateful, but the feeling was mixed with awe. This was a Mazatec Indian who was taking care of me.

Across the river the trail leveled out, the space between the ranges became wider, and little breezes passed by. Whether it was really cooler or not, I don't know, but I began to feel better. By the time we had reached the outskirts of town, I was riding with my head up and managing my own horse.

At the hotel, twelve hours from the time we started, Florrie and I said good-by to Esteban; and, after the necessary arrangements were made, we eased ourselves onto a bed. The hotel didn't serve tea, but we had carried a few leaves with us. We asked for boiling water, threw some leaves into the pan, and drank. We appreciated each sip anew, and after four cups apiece we had the strength to pull off our trail clothes and lie down for a real rest.

The next day we traveled to Tehuacán, and arriving about noon, we wanted dinner. We wanted a good dinner, for we felt we needed it. In search of a restaurant, we stopped in front of a hotel. From the street we could see the dining room—white tablecloths, waiters in white coats serving soup with silver ladles. It looked good, and we were hungry, but it was too high-class for us. We passed on, but came back to walk speculatively past. How rich!

We couldn't resist—we decided to hold up our heads and go in. We had a delicious dinner, and were relieved that no one seemed to consider us out of place.

Our main purpose for going in to Mexico City had been to attend a linguistic conference sponsored by the Mexican Institute of Linguistic Investigation, in conjunction with the Department of Education, the Department of Indian Affairs, the Academies of Aztec and Otomi languages, and the Summer Institute of Linguistics. Members of the various groups were to give papers on some phase of their linguistic research. Among those representing the Summer Institute of Linguistics were: Mr. Townsend speaking on "Analysis and Charting of Morphological Processes"; my brother Ken speaking on "Analysis and Charting of Phonetics, Phonemics and Tonemics"; Florrie speaking on "Notes on the Mazatec Verb"; and I speaking on "Construction and Usage of a Mazatec Primer."

The thought of talking before the conference bigwigs frightened me, but it was the policy of the Summer Institute of Linguistics to share its scientific information with the government and other Mexican organizations, and this seemed to be the time and way to do it.

Mr. Townsend, Ken, and Florrie all did well, and I found that my talk was not as bad as I had expected. Because my Spanish wasn't too good, I spoke through an interpreter, and that procedure did not confuse me as I had feared it would. When I told about the primer, I recounted how Inés had held up her head and said that she was "reading" after her first lesson of three words. That story caught the fancy of one of the Mexican scholars there, and at the close of the meeting he talked about the beauty of it and urged me to put the incident into poetry!

Someone else came bounding up with a different attitude. According to him, my primer was no good, my ideas were no good, and it was nonsense to teach any Indian to read anything but Spanish! He brought over one of the officials of the Mexican government and repeated his objections to him. The official did not agree. Back and forth they argued, talking so fast that I could understand only half of what they said. Finally the official reached over, took the primer out of the professor's hands and bowed low as he handed it back to me. "Go on with your work! It is very good!" Another bow, a smile, and he was gone.

After the conference we rested a little and visited with fellow translators. Then we brought supplies for another stay in Chalco and started back.

As we were passing through Tehuacán we remembered the hotel where we had had the good dinner, and decided to go there again. We went directly to the door, but instead of entering, I felt myself staring from the threshold. I saw the same white tablecloths, the same waiters, the same silver ladles—but they were not rich! The tablecloths were limp and unstarched. The furniture was scuffed, the floor rough and worn. Actually this was one of the poorer hotels. Tehuacán itself had a number of higher grade ones than this.

Even as I sat down and noticed that the silverware

was not really silver, I knew the answer. It was my eyes that had changed, not the hotel. My first visit there had been after nine months in the Mazatec area where my eyes had become accustomed to poverty. On my second visit, the hotel was judged by eyes which had become accustomed to life in Mexico City. Florrie had received similar impressions, and together we laughed at ourselves.

Our eyes had deceived us before. Dresses which had looked all right in Chalco, and which we had thought we would wear in the States, had become impossible by the time we had arrived there. Perhaps if we had watched the advertisements in the papers, our eyes would not have deceived us. We determined that during this stay in Chalco we'd make an effort to remember how the outside world looked.

But we wanted to know what the villages near Chalco were like, too. We would feel more at home if we were familiar with our surroundings. On our walks we made it a point to follow a path for an hour, and then to turn around and go back. On our next walk we chose a different path. In that way we became acquainted with our immediate surroundings, but we wondered what was beyond.

One day Rufina and Silvia invited us to go with them over to the village of Santa Ana to visit their married sister Elena. It was a three-hour walk, and in addition they took us around the village on a sight-seeing tour after we got there. By the time we had walked the three hours back that afternoon, we were ready to fall into bed.

Except for our protesting feet, we had enjoyed

the trip, but perhaps the most interesting thing about it was Marta's reaction to it. When I went for my lesson the next day, she asked me one question after another—when did we start, how long did it take us, did we get tired, whom did we see, and where did we eat? She had been building up to that last question, and I could see that it was more important than any previous ones. I told her that we had eaten with Elena, the sister of Rufina and Silvia. What did we eat—I wondered what was in Marta's mind. I told her that we had eaten chicken in soup, rice, beans, and tortillas. Then Marta asked the question that had been behind the others, "When you ate at Elena's, did she give you a spoon?"

For months Marta had watched us eat with an array of knife, fork, and spoon. She knew that few others in town had any of those tools. But the Sánchez girls were aristocrats, and Elena had put one dessert-size spoon beside each plate. So I could tell Marta, yes, we had a spoon, and she sighed with relief.

Then it was my turn to ask questions. "When you eat you don't use a spoon, do you?"

"No."

"But you don't get your hands wet, do you?"

Oh, oh, that was badly put. Marta's face got red, and it was plain that she was indignant. "Of course not! We don't grab with our hands; we use a tortilla!" (A tortilla is an unleavened corncake; its size and shape are like that of a pancake. When fresh it is firm but pliant, and because it retains its firmness in liquid, it can be used as a scoop. A little piece, torn off, is the Mazatec spoon. A bigger piece wrapped around scrambled eggs takes the place of a fork. With two pieces, one in each hand, meat is torn apart and reduced to manageable size.)

I couldn't apologize to Marta—I took the only way out I knew. "But Marta, you don't get your hands wet because you know how to manage. When I try, the juice from the beans gets on my hands and runs up my sleeve." As I talked I demonstrated, and Marta forgot her indignation and laughed until tears rolled down her face.

Finally she controlled herself enough to say, "That's what children do before they have learned," and she went off into another fit of laughter.

Then she became serious, "But suppose you eat some place where they don't have spoons. What will you do?" I agreed that the situation would be difficult, and asked her to show me how to eat using a tortilla in the place of silverware. To the Mazatecs, tortilla technique is as much a part of good manners as table etiquette is to us.

Sometime later Marta told us of the time she and some of her relatives took a trip to the city of Cordoba. At the restaurant to which they went for dinner, they were given knives, forks, and spoons. They had never used silverware, and they felt that they didn't know how. They were too proud, however, to eat with a tortilla in a place where silverware was provided, so they ate the bread, left the rest, and walked out hungry.

Because of troubles we'd had with tortillas, Florrie and I could sympathize with their problem. We told Marta so, and offered to teach her and her brother to use silverware. With that in mind, we invited each of our neighboring families in for supper. The menu was chosen to fit the occasion—meat to be cut with a knife, vegetables necessitating a fork, and dessert for the spoon. Our friends were shy, and too busy to talk, but they did very well, and probably they gained enough confidence to be willing to try the next time they found a restaurant thus equipped.

The Mazatecs do not always use a tortilla for dipping; frequently they lift their soup to their mouths by means of a piece of bread. This is the favorite way of feeding a young child who is not yet clever with his tortilla. It is also used at banquets. Seldom if ever can the host provide table space for all the guests at a wedding, baptism, or funeral. Of course, as soon as one crowd eats, the tables are reset, but those who have to wait for the third or fourth serving get hungry. To speed up the process, a mother, if she can, sits down at the first serving. As she eats, her child—or two or three of them—comes up behind her chair and nudges her arm. She takes a piece of bread, dips it in her gravy or bean broth, and hands it to him. The little fellow backs away and munches happily.

Seeing the children fed in that way helped me to understand the description of the Last Supper, where in verse 26 of John 13 it says: "Jesus answered, He it is, to whom I shall give a sop, when I have dipped it. And when he had dipped the sop, he gave it to Judas Iscariot, the son of Simon." It had always puzzled me that Jesus, a gentleman, should take a wet piece of bread and hand it to someone. Now, looking at it through Mazatec eyes, I could see that Christ had done a proper and expected thing. He had shared His meal with one of His friends, and had done it in a way approved by those in a culture without knives, forks, and spoons.

But to eat with a tortilla and to dip up gravy with bread was not all that Florrie and I had to learn about food. The day a little girl brought us some luscious-looking honey, we learned about honeycomb. We were delighted, both by the comb honey and by the friendliness of the people who sent it. The little girl listened respectfully while with superlative after superlative we told her how much we enjoyed eating comb honey. She stood around awhile, and I wondered what the trouble was. She stood around some more, and then said, "My father says, as you eat the honey, will you please spit the wax into a paper. He needs it for making candles."

We were slow in the head! We should have known that they'd want the wax back. Paraffin candles were frequently used for lighting, but wax candles were precious, used only for religious purposes. That was the very reason why extracted honey was so cheap (about forty American cents a gallon); people kept bees, not for the honey, but for the wax. Of course, we returned the wax, and hoped that the little girl did not carry the tale of our silly raving.

If the little girl had given us a basketful of oranges instead of honey, she would have answered our thank you with, "It's only two." I felt very proud the first time I remembered to be modest that way. The use of the words "only two" carried over to requests as well. Occasionally, late in the

evening after the stores were closed, Catarina noticed that she had no matches with which to start
the early morning fire. To take care of the emergency, she sent either Tomás or Marcos over to
borrow from us. Usually the request was, "Please,
I need two matches." Only once did I give just two,
and that time I was watching Marcos' face for the
reaction. With an involuntary exclamation he put
out his hand for more; then something in my face
made him withdraw it, and silently he went out.

Mazatecs are as conscious of etiquette as Americans are, and if a person does not come up to stand-
ard he is judged accordingly. I have heard old ladies
chide their grandchildren with, "Don't you know
God? Can't you say 'hello'?" In discussing an outsider, a schoolteacher, or a merchant, the people
may say, "He's a good fellow. He greets us." I have
also heard the reverse. "He's not a good man. He's
conceited. He doesn't talk."

In such an atmosphere, small talk is an essential,
and a few tried and tested phrases an asset.

Perhaps "sit down" is next after "hello" in importance, even though the guest may not respond
until the hostess places the chair for her, or in some
way indicates the place she is expected to sit. Because every welcome guest is seated immediately,
the visitor is told to "sit down" even when greeted
some distance from the house. The guest answers
"thank you," and together the hostess and guest
walk to the house in search of a chair.

As a stranger, and one who must show herself
friendly, I found that small talk paid big dividends,
but was a chore. Frequently we discussed the

weather—the amount of mud on the trails, and their slipperiness—or we discussed prices in the market, we admired the women's embroidery work, or the flowers beside the house.

I was coming back from market one day, and as I passed the home of a friend I called "hello." The woman's baby had been dying of diarrhea a week or two before, and she had brought it to me for medicine. So, as I stood on the trail I asked, "How is your baby?"

"Fine," the mother answered. "That was good medicine."

Then, just for a bit of that essential small talk, I said, "Your baby is pretty."

The mother's response was a modest, "Look at my baby."

But a woman whom I did not know and who was passing on the trail behind me heard my statement, and her response was a laughing cackle, "Let her kill your baby! She says your baby is pretty. Let her kill your baby."

That taught me. I never used that topic for small talk again. The Mazatecs are afraid of the evil eye. Only experience shows who has an evil eye and who hasn't, but the Mazatecs suspect it of all strangers. Their theory is that if a person with an evil eye looks at a baby and desires it, he or she eats the soul of that baby and the baby dies. By calling the baby pretty, I had proved that I desired it, and to the woman who had commented, that spelled his death. The fortunate thing was that I had just saved the baby's life, and the mother was not afraid of me. Her experience with me had demonstrated that I did not have an evil eye.

After that experience, when visiting in the homes of our friends, I listened as the mothers cuddled their babies. "You're ugly! You are very ugly! Aren't you ashamed that you are so ugly?" It startled me to see that not even they themselves would call their babies pretty.

Florrie and I had often noticed the women in the market covering their babies with a shawl as we passed by, and we knew that those women suspected that our eyes were evil. It made us appreciate the confidence of others when for one reason or another they brought their babies to us. We also noticed that their confidence grew the more we learned of their language and their etiquette. And the two, language and etiquette, could not be separated.

CHAPTER IX

In Pursuit of a Dialect

(APRIL, 1939)

PERHAPS MAZATEC, one of the fifty-two aboriginal languages still existing in Mexico, would be termed "relatively unimportant" by many people. Its importance, however, like that of any language, is all in the point of view. A little old Mazatec lady startled Florrie and me with her opinion. She, like many others in the village, was interested in the fact that we were learning her language and that the language we talked between ourselves was not even the same as that of the Mexican schoolteachers. "It is better for you," she said, "that you learn Mazatec. You can walk days in this direction [sweeping the horizon with her hand], and days in that direction [another sweep], and in that and that, and the people still say *ntali* [meaning hello], but no one there speaks your language!"

Florrie and I wondered just how correct the old lady was. That is, over how big an area was the Chalco dialect of Mazatec spoken, and by how many people could it be understood? Specifically, over how large an area, and by how many people, could a New Testament translated into the Chalco dialect of Mazatec be used?

With that question always before us, we developed an almost insatiable curiosity concerning the speech of the surrounding villages. One of our best sources of information was the Mazatec peddlers who traveled from market to market, and it became our habit to ask those with whom we had contact about the places where they had been. At every opportunity we asked, "How do the people of that village talk?"

Among the most common answers were, "We are all one people." (Meaning that the language was the same.) "We understand them, but they mumble their words." (Meaning that there were dialect differences.) Or, "We can't understand them; their language is very hard."

Another source of information was the market itself. The outsiders who wore a costume distinct from that of the Chalco inhabitants were easy to distinguish, and Florrie and I made it a point to seek them out. As we bargained with them for onions or squash, we thought in terms of alphabets—could each of the sounds in their speech be represented by one of the letters we were already using? Would their words be spelled the Chalco way?

Through these sources and others we learned that the dialect in which we were working could be understood throughout most of the area; but according to all reports the speech of one village, Chipango, was completely different from any of the others.

On the map the towns of Chalco and Chipango were side by side and the river which was the boundary line was just an impersonal wiggle between them. Actually the river lay at the bottom of a deep gorge, and because it was almost impassable, centuries had passed with little communication between the two towns. With the river a barrier between them, each dialect had developed independently of the other, until they had become almost mutually unintelligible. In the early 1930's a wire hammock, serving as a foot bridge, had been swung from bank to bank and commerce between the two localities had increased, but their speech differences remained.

Florrie and I had asked so many questions about Chipango that Catarina, whose brother lived there, suggested that we go and see for ourselves what the place was like. She, Esteban, Tomás, and her cousin Adolfo were taking a trip over to the village fiesta, and she invited us to accompany them.

The day before we started, I had been working in the second chapter of Revelation. Because I didn't know the word for "morning star," and because I could not be sure that Catarina had understood when I had described it, I was doubtful of my translation of verse 28, "And I will give him the morning star." Now as we left at 3:15 in the morning, I realized that here was an opportunity to point and ask, "What star is that?" When Adolfo realized that I was interested, he began to tell me about the different stars. Only one star of the southern cross was showing; the others were hidden by the bright moonlight. Using the word Catarina had given me the day before, I asked him to show me the "morning star."

"Khe," said Adolfo as he put into one syllable

our entire sentence of, "It is not up yet."

Catarina had been watching for it, and sometime later she called out. "Look! There's the morning star!"

And there it was, hanging so low over the horizon that it might have been a light shining from a house on the hill. That satisfied me. The word fitted the star and it was apparent that Catarina had understood when I described it to her.

By 8:00 A.M. we had reached the top of the gorge which separated the two towns. Across from us, all we could see was its steep side and below us the river, a mere thread in the distance. The trail, twisting back and forth down the side of the mountain, was too steep for mounted animals. Florrie and I had been trading off, using one horse between us, and Tomás had been riding a donkey. Now we left the animals with the men, and we womenfolk with Tomás started on ahead.

As we walked, the river seemed to be increasing in size. In time, Catarina, whose eyes frequently turned in its direction, stopped us to point out our destination. Following her finger I could see a dark line which cut across the river. Marta's parting words had been, "Be careful when you cross the hammock!" and there it was. I said nothing, but as we went on I wondered just how good a tightrope walker I would prove to be.

The sun had been up for sometime, and now its rays reached to the bottom of the gorge. With each step down there seemed to be less breeze and more heat, and when, after an hour's walk, we were at the river, Florrie and I were glad to stretch out and rest.

Travelers coming from the other direction were also there, and they stared at us in amazement. They wanted to know what "white-headed women" were doing in that area and why. From where we lay we could hear Esteban's answer to their questions and listened while he supplied additional information. With a studied air of indifference, trying to conceal the pride he felt, he told them that we spoke the Mazatec language. The exclamation of awe that followed that announcement satisfied even Esteban, while Florrie and I felt ashamed of how little we actually knew.

The men had been working while they talked, preparing to carry the packs across the river. The hammock to be used as a bridge was made from two cables stretched from one side of the river to the other. Wires about a foot apart made up a V-shaped net which hung down from the cables. In order to clear the river in spite of the sag, the cables had been slung from trees high on the bank. Seen close at hand, the hammock was not as alarming as Marta had led us to believe. Actually the net was about four feet deep, and poles had been laid at the bottom of it to facilitate walking. Except for those places where the poles had fallen out and the wires themselves were the only footing, the hammock seemed quite secure.

Florrie and I watched while, with the packs hanging from their heads, the men started across. Holding on to the sides of the net, they steadied themselves against the hammock's swing, and by walking slowly and carefully they kept the bounce at a minimum.

Florrie and I were afraid that our shoes would slip on the round poles or wires; so when we crossed we took off our shoes and walked in our stocking feet. Florrie and I had less to fear than Catarina did, for both of us could swim, but looking through the hammock at the river below we knew that we would not care to fall in either. The brown water was flowing swiftly but silently.

Once on the other side, we stood by to see the animals come. The different travelers were helping each other, and at this time there were three men on one bank and two on the other. They doubled a rope back across the river, tied one end around the horse's neck, and drove him into the water. After five or six steps he went down out of sight and the men on our side of the river began to pull. Where was that horse! Would he ever come up! I hurried back out on the hammock where I could watch the river. At last the horse appeared. Shaking with fright, he set his feet on solid ground and was unwilling to move them, even when the men tried to pull him to the bank. The donkeys were out of sight even longer than the horse, but it did not bother them. They came out, shook their ears, and stood waiting for their packs to be put on again.

All in all, with a lunch, a rest, and a swim for the men, three hours had passed and it was twelve o'clock noon before we were on our way again. Although the grade was more gradual than it had been on the other side, we had to climb out of the same ravine into which we had dropped. Whew! The sun was hot and each step was an effort. With only one horse between Florrie and me, the one riding was continually concerned for the one walking. Each of us tried to put on a tough front when, after sizing up the condition of the other, we offered to walk. Our "toughness" fooled no one, and as though we had been children, Catarina urged us on with, "We can't stop here; there's no shade." Esteban kept promising, "Just a little farther; then we'll rest."

Ten minutes after leaving the river, we had left big trees that made good shade. From where we were we could see only shrubs and bushes, and I wondered why Esteban and Catarina insisted that we go on—was one bush better than another? Perhaps dropping into the gorge had made us mountain sick. Perhaps the hot sun had weakened us. We wanted nothing more than a chance to rest, but we kept on. I had been walking, head down, trying to keep my rebellious stomach under control, when an exclamation from Florrie made me look up. There was our shade! It was made by beautiful *chicozapote* and mango trees, and beneath them a rivulet tumbled across the path. No words were needed. We put our arms in the water and wet our faces and heads. The water felt so good and the ground so nice and soft—I suppose that was the first time the Lord had ever been thanked for that specific clump of trees and water. Catarina, Esteban, Adolfo—all of us—lay down and I at least went to sleep.

By three o'clock we were beginning to stretch—

we had covered the distance from the river to the
mango trees in forty-five minutes; silly to have tired
so quickly—and by four we were on our way again.
As we traveled Florrie's and my self-respect came
back; we found that we could walk along as fast
as our companions cared to.

It was around seven o'clock and getting dark
when we reached the village. The appearance of the
town differed from that of Chalco in that the houses
were not as tall, and the low roofs made them look
like piles of hay. To Florrie and me the thick sugar-
cane thatch of Chalco was more beautiful, but our
companions preferred the straw of Chipango. Straw,
they said, lasted twenty years as a roof, whereas
sugar-cane leaf lasted about ten.

The men stayed with the animals while Florrie
and I hurried after Catarina down through the
center of town. When she stopped, her flashlight
played over a little hut tucked up against a bank.
It was her brother's house, but there was no light
and no sign of a fire. Catarina called a trial "Hello,"
and her sister-in-law answered inviting us in. Once
inside, we understood the lack of light and fire. The
sister-in-law was in bed with a baby, only a few days
old, and her husband was not yet home from work.

Florrie and I sat on chairs at one end of the hut
while Catarina talked to the mother. The flashlight
was still on, and as Catarina talked it jerked, showing us the hearth with its charred wood and the
ever-present stones, three of them set to hold the
cooking bowl above the fire; another jerk and we
saw clothes hanging from pegs in the corner. An
eight-year-old girl, followed by her four-year-old sis-

ter, came over to take her mother's place as hostess.

For a few minutes Catarina and her sister-in-law chatted; then, Catarina, after being on the road from 3:15 in the morning until 7:00 at night, after walking all the way, put on her apron and went to work. Slowly, calmly, with no fuss nor flutter, she lighted a candle, swept up the ashes, started a fire, put on a pot for coffee; and the dark hovel became home.

As the twilight outside changed to night, Augustín, Catarina's brother, and his two sons came in. Esteban and Adolfo, who had fed and sheltered the animals, now sat on chunks of wood discussing the price of corn with Augustín. Two other men came in, but neither the coals under the clay pot, nor the flickering candle gave me enough light to see what they looked like. The candle didn't have much of a chance, for the dark dirt floor, the brown unpainted walls, the smoke-covered rafters absorbed rather than reflected its light. It wasn't a real candle anyway; it was made from a tin can, a tin tube, a pop bottle cap, and a rag. As the kerosene burned, the light flickered and hard fine soot was given off, but it was cheaper than the more conventional candle and therefore was used by most Mazatecs. The flashlight had been turned off to be used again only when more light was needed than that supplied by the candle.

Probably the candlelight was kinder to our surroundings than electricity would have been, and probably it was more restful. Except for Catarina at the fire, no one tried to work; we sat, sipping coffee and eating bread.

When we had finished, Augustín got out a big straw mat and without comment laid it on the floor. Florrie and I knew that the mat was our bed, but we had never been in that situation before, and we did not know what was expected of us. Well, the time had come for something. The whole household seemed to be waiting, half-embarrassed, half-curious. They knew that we slept in a bed, but they had no bed to offer us and they wondered what we would do. Catarina helped us out, "I'm going to bed," she said, walking to the mat. One minute she was standing and the next she was down. The only difference between "in bed" and "out of bed" was that of position. Florrie and I followed her, but we had a middle position in between our vertical and horizontal one; we sat while taking off our shoes.

Then we played possum under our blankets for what seemed hours while the rest of the house was settling. Again and again a flashlight shone in our faces while some whispered, "Look! They're asleep!"

At last the candle was blown out and all was quiet. Cautiously I raised myself up on my elbow. I wanted to see who my housefellows were. I had already made the acquaintance of some fleas; while supposedly sleeping I had let them eat their fill. The moonlight came in through the cracks in the walls, and by means of it I could see the people stretched out on all sides of me. Tomás, between us and Catarina, was sleeping quietly; Esteban beyond was a bit noisier; others, bumps under blankets, were breathing in various rhythms. The sound of it snatched me back to the hospital. I was on night duty and after a few hard hours had succeeded in getting my patients to sleep. Content, I lay down again, and ignoring the hard floor and aching hips, I managed to sleep.

Toward morning, light crept in the cracks of the walls and under the straw roof. That was all the little four-year-old needed, and she started to talk to her sister. Gruffly her daddy hushed her. A little later Florrie whispered in my ear. We'd get up and go outside before the others were awake. Quietly we reached for our shoes, but that one movement was enough. As one man the household arose. That time they were the ones who had been playing possum.

We wanted to wash our hands and faces, but since there was no water in the house, we accompanied the women as they went for some. The entire village used two springs at the bottom of a gully, and at ordinary times that was sufficient; but the fiesta had tripled the population, and this was dry season. The water seeped out of the bank so slowly that women stood in line for hours waiting for an opportunity to fill their jars. When Florrie and I saw the situation, we were ashamed to ask for wash water; so we waited until the next morning and then rubbed our faces and hands with leaves wet with dew.

We even hesitated about asking for more coffee, when the number of visitors in Augustín's house increased to twenty. Although we were in the same household, we never once sat down to eat as a family. We couldn't have, for there were only two chairs and four cups and plates. People drifted in and

out, and as soon as one finished eating another
started.

When it was Florrie's and my turn to eat, Catarina, who knew that at home we used knife, fork,
and spoon, quietly put the tortillas and juicy beans
in front of us and left. Now we were in the position
Marta had said we would be some day. Our food
was in front of us, and we had no silverware with
which to eat it. We managed, but not without
getting our hands wet. The next meal was the same.
The meal after that, tactful Catarina served the
beans dry and between tortillas sandwich style.

Catarina remembered, too, that we had taken
the trip because we wanted to hear the dialect. She
told her brother and he arranged for a woman to
study with us. We found that frequently names of
things were pronounced the same in both towns,
but most of the verbs differed beyond recognition.

By the end of the second day we had decided that
the people of Chipango would not be able to use the
New Testament as translated into the Chalco dialect; they would need another translation of their
own. The picture was not entirely black, however,
for the dialects were enough alike so that knowledge of one would help us to assimilate the other
when the time came for us to work on it.

We didn't limit our language study to those hours
which we spent with the informant. Whenever we
went for water, or took a walk, we spoke to the
people and listened as they answered. As we stood
in line at the water hole, we touched a leaf, a stone,
a jar, anything in sight, and said the Chalco name
for the thing we touched. To the women it was

almost a game, and they responded by giving us the Chipango word for the object. As we met the women on the paths, they responded to our greeting with "Hello, Miss Chalco." I liked that. In Chalco many people were doubtful of our origin; we were mythical somebodies from somewhere. In Chipango we had been located as from Chalco!

At 2:00 P.M. of the third day, we said good-by to our Chipango friends and started home. A thick layer of clouds kept off the sun and we traveled faster than we had on our trip over. In fact, the trail seemed so easy that we were amazed at how quickly we reached the rivulet where we had rested previously. By 4:30 we were at the hammock. Nothing seemed as bad this time as it had on the way over. Our traveling companions did not seem as tired either, and within an hour the packs and animals were across the river. Without waiting any longer, Catarina, Tomás, Florrie, and I started to walk up the side of the gorge. After climbing about a third of the way, we came out of the brush and could look back at the river. Soon the others reached that point too, and we could see that the horse was tired and still frightened from the river. He walked a few steps and stopped to rest, a few more and he stopped again. Because the men chose to keep a steady pace, they passed him, whistling for him to follow.

For a while the horse did, but with each stop it chose to rest longer. When at last Florrie, Catarina, Tomás and I had reached the highest loop, Esteban with the donkeys was on the loop below, and one loop farther down Adolfo was sitting, waiting for

the horse to catch up. After a bit he decided that
his whistling was doing no good; but instead of
going down to get the horse, he worked his way
over until he was standing above it. From there
he threw rocks, making them land just behind the
horse. Startled, the animal moved and finally caught
up with the rest of us.

It was dark when we arrived at a sugar-cane mill,
a place where the sap is pressed out and the juice
made into sugar or liquor. The owners welcomed
us and brought in some supper—not beans this time,
but goat meat. As usual, the people gave us the best
they had. This time the best they had to sleep on
was made from sugar-cane pulp, the stalks which
were left after the juice had been squeezed out.
They laid the straw mat on top of it, and compared
to the ground this bed felt like an innerspring mattress.

When we went to bed, our party agreed that we
would get up at the second crow of the rooster. At
midnight he crowed, and in a whisper Esteban and
Adolfo reassured each other that that was only the
first time. About 3:30 when he crowed again, our
hostess blew on the embers and started the fire for
coffee, and Esteban fed the horses. Florrie and I lay
"on bed" and listened to the donkeys munching
their breakfast. One advantage of being up when
you stand up is that you don't have to get up until
you are ready to go. We got up, had our coffee, and
were off by 4:30 A.M.

The rest of the trip was uneventful. Tomás expressed the sentiments of all of us when, nearing
Chalco, he whacked his donkey and called, "Come

on! Come on! Hurry up! We're almost there, back
to the land where we were born."

Florrie and I echoed his sentiment. True it was
only two and a half years since we had first seen
Chalco. True too that the customs were strange,
and that we were still struggling to understand their
language and to be understood, but compared to
Chipango, Chalco was home.

CHAPTER X

Beliefs

(MAY — JULY, 1939)

DISHWASHING TIME at our house became a favorite part of the day for Tomás and our other neighbors. They learned that though Florrie and I were busy with our hands, our minds were free for a chat. They leaned against the table which held the dishpan, or sat close by. Some days we explained where kerosene came from, how people were kept from starvation in a land where snow made winter gardens impossible, and that the ocean was much, much bigger than a river. Usually before the dishes were finished, someone had asked that we all sing the Mazatec version of "Jesus Loves Me," or Tomás' favorite, "Brighten the Corner." Usually, too, someone requested that we teach them a Bible verse. So we studied a new one together, and then listened while each one recited a verse which he had learned previously. Inés and Tomás chose from a memorized group of ten or more, while some of the others stumbled shyly through the only verse they knew.

No matter where Tomás was, the verses which he had learned bubbled out. He went to a funeral, sat in the kitchen, and recited all he knew. Urged on by the women who were preparing the funeral feast, he said them again and again. Catarina happily told us about it later. "The women say that God's Word is beautiful." At last a Mazatec was spreading "the good news"! Florrie and I were glad, but surprised too, for we hadn't expected that the first messenger would be a six-year-old boy.

Tomás was confident of a home in Heaven, and he frequently questioned us concerning it. In one of his thoughtful moods he asked, "When I go to Heaven, how will I go? Will I fly like a buzzard, up, up, up?" We had to admit that we didn't know what his mode of transportation would be, and he continued to gaze thoughtfully at the buzzards.

One day he was sent on an errand and as he passed a house with a fierce dog, the dog rushed at him, tore his shirt, and left teeth marks on his chest. As I put disinfectant on his wound, I asked him, "Did the owner come out?"

"No."

"Then what made the dog leave?"

"God sent an angel and drove him away," he answered seriously.

In real life, Bible stories were a comfort to him, and in his play the characters were almost companions.

One day Marcos started playfully toward him with a growl, "I'm a lion!"

With a shrug of indifference Tomás answered, "You can't hurt me. I'm Daniel."

Marcos' arms dropped and the game was over.

Another of Tomás' playmates was Zita, a cousin of Inés. When I wondered which of them was the older, Inés assured me that they were about the same age because "their teeth are falling out at the same time."

Zita too was learning Bible verses, and among them Revelation 1:5: "Unto him that loved us, and washed us from our sins in his own blood." Because the verse did not actually mention Christ's name, I wanted to be sure that she knew who it was that loved her. Frequently after she had repeated the verse I would ask, "Who is it who loves you?"

"Jesus," she would answer. Perhaps I asked too many times, for she felt the need to tell me once and for all, "Jesus loves me, and He doesn't hate me even the teeniest weeniest little bit!"

As soon as Zita had learned to say Revelation 1:5 and John 3:16 without help, we suggested that she tell the verses to her mother. Later Inés remonstrated with us, "Don't tell Zita to say the Bible verses to her mother. They make her mother angry, and she spanks her for it." We remembered that the Lord had not promised an easy time for His followers, but it bothered Florrie and me that our zeal may have caused Zita trouble, and we were awed that the first Mazatec to be punished for propagating the Gospel was a cute little girl. We were surprised, too, for seldom did a Mazatec object to the Bible; most of them, like the women cooking at the funeral, enjoyed listening.

The Mazatecs' listening was made easier as our ability to speak improved, and they became more willing to talk of matters close to their hearts when our understanding improved. They had remained silent rather than speak slowly and loudly of their private affairs. Occasionally they spoke once and if we did not understand, the chance was gone; they did not repeat. When we could follow a fast conversation, we could more easily acquire knowledge of their beliefs and attitudes.

We had associated with them long enough to suspect that their basic beliefs were not represented by the big moss-covered church that stood in the town square. Nor were they represented by the saint pictures which occupied a shelf in almost every house in town. Once these pictures had been set in place, they were for the most part ignored, and from quick words spoken when the people were musing or frightened, we received hints of other beliefs.

Catarina had been frightened, not only by the earthquake which shook the house as we studied one day, but because of the personality associated with it. Quickly she spoke, "I wonder what he wants."

"Who?" we asked her.

"Father Earthquake." Then she explained. "When an earthquake comes, it is because Father Earthquake wants sickness, or a corn famine, or perhaps a big storm." Our explanation of an earthquake seemed to be no comfort to her; she listened, but as one interested in the activities of "Father Earthquake."

We had heard the title "Father" applied to the sun and the moon, but perhaps we had considered it as part of a name similar to our English "daddy longlegs."

Then one evening we stood in our doorway chatting with Ida. She was one who had a habit of asking us questions; and in the same manner as she sought information on airplanes and trains, she looked up at the bright moon and asked, "What is Father Moon like? Is he living?"

By her question and the expression on her face, we knew that for her the moon was more than an object in the sky, and the title "Father" had been used with respect. We suspected that her question had been influenced by our teaching, for we had emphasized that God is alive and powerful. By analogy she was questioning the moon, and our explanation that the moon's light is reflected from the sun seemed to satisfy her.

Marcos had never questioned us about the moon nor about the sun, but he had been in our house almost every day, and we had supposed that he knew that God had made the sun. His lack of understanding became apparent when he saw an eclipse of the sun. He ran in to Florrie exclaiming, "Father Sun and Father Moon are fighting!"

"Don't say 'Father Sun,'" Florrie objected. "The sun is not God."

"What do you mean, 'the sun isn't God'?" demanded Marcos. "Doesn't God's Word say, 'I am the light of the world'?" And so it did. One of the verses we had helped him to memorize was John 8:12. Unsuccessfully Florrie tried to explain the eclipse, and the meaning of John 8:12; and because we were afraid that others would interpret the passage as Marcos had, we no longer taught that verse to beginners.

We learned to be more careful about identifying God, and to make sure that the people knew whom we were talking about. We told them parts of the first chapter of Genesis and emphasized that God made the sun, that it was His property, and that the sun was not God. Many Mazatecs had listened without emotion to our teachings from Acts 4:12, that "only Jesus can save us, not the images, not money." When we added, "It is not right for us to worship the sun," some of them were surprised but accepted our statement. Others objected, "But without Father Sun, our corn would not grow!"

The argument of one of the more intelligent women was, "The priest says the sun is God!"

We didn't believe that he would have said such a thing. "Surely you misunderstood him," we told her.

"You've seen the images in the church?" she asked.

"Yes."

"Well, why would each one have a halo if they had not come down from the sun?"

We remained silent. How could we explain to a sunworshipper that the halo on an image did not indicate a connection between it and the sun?

For years a priest had said mass in that church, but perhaps because he spoke Spanish and the people spoke Mazatec, his teachings had gone astray. Most of the customs which so obviously had been taught by the church were merely a veneer covering up the old tribal beliefs. The outsider saw the veneer and was unaware of those beliefs which lay closest to the heart of the Mazatec.

We wondered if the priest himself was aware of the confidence which the Mazatecs had in the mushroom—not just any mushroom, but a special kind they called affectionately "Little Holy Mushroom." It was Ramón, Marta's brother, who first told us about it. He told us that when a person ate the mushroom he saw visions of what was going to happen, and that Jesus Himself talked to him. Not everybody dared eat it, because if a bad person ate the mushroom it killed him instead of helping him. The mushroom was eaten at night because Jesus wouldn't talk unless it was dark.

By the expression on our faces, Ramón saw that we doubted the connection between Jesus and the mushroom. He insisted, "I know the rich people don't use the mushroom. Jesus gave it as a special gift to us poor people. He gave it to us because we don't have money to pay a doctor when sick."

"Does the mushroom help the sick?"

"Yes. Some people get well immediately."

We found the belief in the mushroom to be very widespread among the Mazatecs. A sentimental interest in the butterfly was less so, but was real to some people. Interest in the butterfly centered around the celebration of All Saints' Day. On that day and on the day preceding it, the people burned candles in the cemetery and some went to mass; but they also prepared a feast, for that was the time of the year, according to Mazatec belief, that the dead were released from jail and allowed to return home for a visit. The people spent their hoarded money and loaded the table with the goodies the dead ones had liked best. In deference to the church a picture of the Virgin of Guadalupe was on most of the feast tables, and candles burned in front of it, but it was the action of the butterflies that charmed at least some of the Mazatec households.

Butterflies, especially abundant at this season, entered the house to rest on the food, lightly fanning their wings. No one disturbed them, for might not they be the souls of loved ones? Sometimes when the door stood ajar, the butterflies, ignoring the food, rested in the sunshine on the floor, seeming to enjoy the atmosphere of the home. All Saints' Day passed and the dead supposedly went back to jail again. The fiesta was over, the food was eaten, and in a few days most of the butterflies had disappeared.

We could see no line of demarcation between the old tribal beliefs and the new religion superimposed by the Spanish conquerors. It seemed to us that the superimposed beliefs had been accepted with complete lack of understanding, and the Mazatecs had applied them in strange ways. One of the ways became apparent as I treated the children's sores. In Chalco where disinfectants had been almost unknown, the children had frequent infections. Many times a stubbed toe, a scratch from a stick, the bite of an insect, turned into an oozing sore. When the children came to me, I cleaned up the spot, put on a disinfectant, and covered it with a patch. It seemed to me that the bandage fell off in no time; and to make it stick better, I used two pieces of adhesive, crossing them at the site of the sore. The place healed; but until I changed my procedure and used parallel strips of adhesive, it was the "cross" that received the credit, not the medicine.

For the most part I enjoyed treating the children's

sores, for they healed quickly and the children were delighted with the help received, but the people who came to me with tuberculosis discouraged me. There seemed to be little I could do for them.

We hadn't even been able to help Catarina's sister. We had known when we moved up to Catarina's house that Tomás' mother was sick, but not until later did we realize that she had tuberculosis. After we had moved in, we heard her coughing, coughing— she died about six months later. Tomás' baby sister Frida was sick too. Catarina had had the care of her for some time, and usually held her in her arms while we studied. The baby became thinner and thinner. She died about six weeks after her mother.

The baby's funeral was not a big one, and only Catarina felt the death deeply. She had no children of her own, and had counted heavily on Frida. One man balanced the casket on his shoulder while we walked slowly from the house to the cemetery. The women carried candles and flowers, and a man followed along shooting off firecrackers.

For the most part we walked quietly, but Frida's father, Vicente, was a disturbing element. He was an alcoholic, perpetually drunk; he had left his wife, his daughter, and his son Tomás in the care of Catarina and Esteban. Now the wife and daughter were dead, and his own body so debilitated by liquor that he himself was to live less than six months more. Even as we walked he wanted a drink, but he had nothing with him. In a heavy whisper he urged Tomás to leave the procession, go home, get the bottle and bring it to him. Catarina interrupted to say that returning would make Tomás late, and he was not to go. The boy obeyed Catarina rather than his father, but the nagging for a drink continued all the way to the cemetery.

From a distance the cemetery was brown and barren, while close at hand the brownness took on bumps, sharp mounds over graves too close together to permit me to place a foot between them. I stopped trying and stepped, like those with me, directly on the mounds. At the end of each mound was a wooden cross, some new, some weather-beaten. The ground was so crowded that the graves were emptied periodically and bones, hair, anything that remained of the coffin and its occupant, were dumped at the foot of a big central cross. As we passed that cross, I was fascinated by the skulls. After I remembered to look away, I was embarrassed —someone may have noticed and wondered why I looked so long. We passed the graves of some of the wealthier, with the cement coffin-like monument taking the place of the dirt mound. I didn't ask, but I wondered if the purpose of such a gravestone might not be a protection against the evacuation process.

The hole which had been dug for Frida was a big one, made wide in the search of vacant space. The coffins seemed to be on different levels, some separated from others by boards or masonry.

We gathered around the grave, and the men prepared to lower the coffin. Vicente insisted on helping, and got into the hole ready to receive it. Reluctantly the men started to hand the coffin to him. Then, as it was almost in his hands, he stopped them, dug around in his pockets for a match, lit a cigarette, and with it between his lips he again reached for his daughter.

From where I stood I could see the ends of several coffins, and one had been removed to make room for Frida. As soon as she was in, the other coffin was to be placed back on top. Vicente slid Frida into place and then studied the old coffin. It had a special feature, a glass window cut in the cover. As he studied it, he mumbled, "That's my son Pablo." (Catarina had told me that Tomás' brother had died as a baby.) Vicente leaned forward and peered through the window. For a long time he gazed, then straightening, and looking up at us collected around the grave, he announced, "He is still in existence." I recoiled with repugnance at his hardness and the implication that existence was dependent upon a few dry bones.

We were constantly trying to teach the people about Heaven and existence after death, and a number of children had memorized Revelation 21:4: "And God shall wipe away all tears from their eyes; and there shall be no more death, neither sorrow, nor crying, neither shall there be any more pain: for the former things are passed away." But with that verse we told them that not everyone arrived at the beautiful place, for Christ had said, "No man cometh unto the Father, but by me." And many of our friends memorized John 14:6.

Perhaps because of the verses, we gained a reputation throughout the town as being, in some vague way, "authorities on religion." Because of this reputation even people we did not know occasionally came to the house to ask questions about spiritual things. That was what brought a teenage fellow to see us one evening. He had been reading a Spanish Gospel of John and the third chapter had puzzled him.

"Is it true," he asked, "that we must be born again?"

"Yes, that's what the Bible tells us."

"What does a person look like who has been born a second time?" His eyes never left my face as I tried to explain.

"It's his heart or soul that looks different. When a person believes in Christ, Christ gives him a new heart, exchanging the heart which had only death for the one that has eternal life." And I added, "If you believe in Jesus, you yourself are born again."

He was not quite satisfied. "Can even murderers enter Heaven?" That question was one I'd been asked before; murder was frequent in Chalco.

"Yes. Even a murderer, if he believes in Christ, can enter Heaven, because then Christ takes his guilt upon Himself. Of course, if the man really believes, he won't commit murder again. He will want to do what is right." That satisfied him and he began to wonder what Heaven would be like.

"Do men plant corn up there?"

"The Bible doesn't say, but we know that we will have everything we need." He stayed a little longer, and his questions made us wish that we could put a Mazatec New Testament into his hands and say, "Here, read it!" Some day, if we kept on struggling, maybe we could.

CHAPTER XI

"Lo, I Am with You Alway"

(AUGUST, 1939 — APRIL, 1953)

EVENTUALLY—YEARS LATER—we did have whole sections of Scripture to put into the hands of our Mazatec friends. The Gospel of Mark was published in 1946, and with the arrival of the books the character of our work changed slightly. Time spent at the desk lessened, while we spent more time teaching from the Gospel and helping people to read it.

Eduardo was among the first twenty to buy a copy, but that was not an indication of wealth. He had less worldly goods than most of the young men we knew. He had not inherited land, and land is frequently the measure of a Mazatec's riches. In order to support his mother and sister, he did the work of a hired man for one of our wealthier neighbors. The neighbors, with no loss of pride, could beg us for tin cans, picture books, anything that struck their fancy. Not so Eduardo; if we offered him one of the very cans that they had been begging for, he would refuse it with a short "No." Was he proving to himself that he was rich enough to turn down a can, we wondered?

They reacted to the Gospel of Mark as they had done to tin cans. We were trying to sell the books, but the more well-to-do people thought they should be given one. They had a variety of reasons: they had rented a pack animal to us, or they had given us a gift of stewed beans, or they felt themselves to be our very special friends. In contrast to this, Eduardo walked in with his money and, with no argument, he bought a copy.

Even after the people had their books, differences between Eduardo and the others continued. The others were dependent on us as they read. We picked out the easier passages for them and showed them *what* to read. We showed them *how* to read, for instead of puzzling over a difficult word they would turn to us for help. Almost we showed them *when* to read; that is, they read when they came to our house or when we called on them; we hoped that they read at other times too, but we doubted it.

Eduardo himself chose what he would read. He preferred to start at the beginning, and he had no interest in jumping around to the more easily understood portions. If we turned to one of those parts, he sat silent until we had turned back to his chosen place.

The first fifteen verses of Mark are good, but we felt almost desperate about them when day after day that was all he would read. He wanted to know them perfectly; and he would not consent, even for a little while, to skip ahead and read about Christ's crucifixion or resurrection. He wouldn't even go on to the next page, to verses 23 through 27, to read about Christ's casting out the unclean spirit.

Eventually we gave in to his independent spirit and stopped trying to guide his reading. Meekly we listened as he went through chapter 1, verses 1 through 15, correcting him whenever he made a mistake and supplying the word whenever his sharp, "What does that say?" showed that he anticipated trouble.

The day came when he read those fifteen verses perfectly, and then he consented to turn to the next page. I was pleased that he did so well, but he hadn't finished even the first chapter before he stood up and the session was over.

And he didn't come back, at least not for help in Mark.

But apparently he was reading at home. His boss, who stumbled and stuttered his way through a page, told us that Eduardo was doing well. Others, ashamed that a hired man was beating them at reading, took pains to tell us that he had had more schooling than they had. We listened, remembered how easily information offered was tailored to fit the circumstances, and remained of the opinion that the difference in progress was due to attitude and hard work, not to past advantages. But if Eduardo was really studying the Gospel, he'd need another book soon, and we hoped that he was just one of many who were already looking forward to more Scripture.

Florrie had done most of the work on the Gospel of Mark, and a more ordinary woman might have thought her translation work finished with that book. She had married George Cowan, a fellow translator, and by 1944 there was a little Cowan to love and care for. But not even a family turned Florrie aside from the task the Lord had given her.

With one eye on little Paul, or on dinner as it cooked on the stove, Florrie continued her work with the First Epistle of John and with Acts.

Acts is needed by any new growing church. And the First Epistle of John is packed with truths pertinent to the Mazatecs. It states very clearly that we are saved through belief in Christ, and that believing we are sons of God. It also has a sterner message: "He that loveth not his brother abideth in death" and "Whosoever hateth his brother is a murderer: and ye know that no murderer hath eternal life abiding in him."

The Mazatecs needed both types of messages. Many welcomed the message that Jesus Christ intercedes for us with God the Father, even while they were cheating their brothers out of their inheritance, and perhaps intending to kill them for it. We wanted the First Epistle of John in order to teach them that "we know him, if we keep his commandments."

When the completed books reached us in 1949, my new partner, Sarah Gudschinsky, and I turned our energies into their distribution. Eduardo heard that they had arrived, and he came to the house to buy a copy of each. I was curious to know how much progress he had made; so I said, "Read to me, will you?" Usually he was very serious, but at my request a pleased little smile caused the corners of his mouth to twitch. Then with dignity he opened the book of Acts, and although he had never had a copy before he read it fluently.

I wondered if he had become to believe in the Lord, and I wanted to point out some of the comforting verses of First John. When I tried to do so, however, his independent spirit showed itself again, and he left for home.

His home was one of the poorest in the village; it was tiny, with big cracks at the corners and between the boards of the wall. Sarah and I frequently went calling to encourage and help those people who were interested in reading, and to teach a hymn or a Bible verse to those who thought they were incapable of reading.

In the course of time Sarah happened to stop at Eduardo's home. He was away working, but his mother and sister were there and received her cordially. As we habitually did when visiting, Sarah took the opportunity to tell them about the Lord. "That's what Eduardo says!" they agreed.

After she had received that response to several of her explanations, Sarah asked, "How does Eduardo know?"

With no hesitation his mother answered, "He studies those books he bought from you."

When the Cowans and I were told of her response, we rejoiced at the proof that the Mazatec translation, although not perfect, was good enough so that a man could read it, learn about the Lord from it, and pass its message on to his loved ones.

But Eduardo wouldn't let us subside into a feeling of complacency. He was one of those who kept at us with, "Don't you have anything new?"

Sarah and I had been revising the primers, and making up stories whose vocabularies were restricted to the easier words. Our purpose was to teach the people to read the simple books, in the hope that through them they would gain the ability and confidence to read Scripture.

But Eduardo was not interested in the easier things. "Don't you have the Gospel of John?" he asked.

"George and Florrie are working on it," we told him. Then we tried to explain to him why it took so long.

But he wasn't interested in the details, and he interrupted with, "When will it be ready?"

Some of the Old Testament stories that Sarah and I had prepared appeased him for a while, but the next time he saw us he asked, "When will the New Testament be finished?"

We knew it would be years before the New Testament was ready, but we longed for him to have it. He needed it if he were to be a well-rounded Christian. As we tried to think of a way to supply his need, we remembered his persistence and studious habits. Would it be possible, we wondered, for him to get help from the Spanish New Testament?

The next time he asked us for a Mazatec New Testament, we handed him a copy in Spanish. He took it and for half an hour he sat studying, dipping into it here and there. Then abruptly he stood up and handed it back. "I can't understand it. I'll wait until it is translated into my language."

Of course he was right. The New Testament in a language not his own, and in which he understood only a smattering of words, would be a poor substitute for a New Testament in the language of his home. We didn't urge him to take the Spanish

Testament; instead we asked the Lord to help us to complete the Mazatec one.

Even while we were concerned for Eduardo and other Christians who were restricted to Mark, Acts, and First John, we remembered those Mazatecs who, as yet, did not have even the book of Mark. The Lord's message to us is, "Go ye into all the world, and preach the gospel to every creature." Although we had left the United States and had gone to Chalco, we could not feel that His orders had been completed. There were still villages beyond Chalco that had not heard, and they were also included in the "world." The Lord intended that they, too, should hear. So, by 1953, we were spending much of our time tramping the mountains, going to the village markets, introducing and selling the books there.

Some of the markets were a three-hour walk away, and since we liked to be there by nine o'clock, we frequently were up and on the trail by six. We went early in order to sell the books quickly and start home again before too many of the men had had time to become drunk and bothersome.

The market of Rio de Flores, like that of other towns, hummed with excitement the first time we entered it. The people watched us walk in, and even though we each had a basketful of books, they wondered why we had come. They hung back, waiting to see what we would do. We felt shy too, but to indulge in one's shyness was no way to sell books. Sarah smiled and opened one for a group of women to see, while I walked up to a group of men.

Curiosity conquered. They wanted to see what

our books were like. They watched and listened while we read them bits from the story of the Creation, the story of the Flood, or portions from Mark, Acts, and First John. We also showed them a "dictionary." It had only a thousand words, but they liked it because it gave a Spanish word for each Mazatec word, and by using it they could learn Spanish. No one bought immediately; instead they stood around and discussed the books among themselves. Then one man stepped forward and bought a dictionary. The ice was broken and others followed his example. Some of them bought Scripture, while some bought primers or Bible stories.

This market was so small that we could go from group to group and give everyone a chance to look at the books and hear a portion of Scripture. As we were leaving, we stopped at the edge of the market and glanced back over the crowd; then satisfied that we had overlooked no one, we turned down the trail for home. Knowing that a three-hour hike lay ahead of us, we were glad that our baskets were lighter than when we had come.

We were about halfway between the two towns when we met an old lady traveling alone. "Where are you going?" she asked us.

"We are selling books," we replied with our usual answer to that question. That answer not only gave a reason for our presence in out-of-the-way places, but frequently it was the wedge for a new sale.

"What are they like?" she asked. I took a book from my basket, while she, turning sideways, rested her pack on a boulder beside the trail. Then slowly she eased herself out from under its carrying rope.

"Sit down!" she insisted, glad for an excuse to rest. Her friendliness to tall, white-skinned strangers surprised us, but we welcomed the chance to talk with her. As the path was just a lane between stones, we stopped where we were, and sat on those stones which happened to be arranged in a convenient circle.

We chose the story of Creation, for we suspected that she was a sun-worshiper; most Mazatecs were. She couldn't read, but we let her hold the book as we turned the pages for her. While she looked at the pictures, we told her that the real God made the world and everything in it. One of the things He made was the sun; the sun itself was without thoughts, without goodness, without badness. She listened carefully, but everything we said she reinterpreted in her old traditional way of thinking.

"Jesus Christ is the Son of the real God," we told her.

Her response was a fervent, "Jesus Christ! Holy Mary! Father Sun lights our way. We'd walk in the dark if it were not for him."

We told her, "The real God made not only the trees, fish, birds, animals, and man, but He made the sun too."

She responded, "Father Sun is taking care of us. We are in his hands."

Then happy that she had found a paper which talked about her "Little Father," she dug down into her pack for twenty centavos with which to buy it. As she was hunting, I thumbed through the Creation story and prayed, "Lord, I'm telling this old lady, but only You can make her understand."

She found her money, paid for the book, and then carefully retied her pack for travel. When she had finished, she looked up and asked, "What is Heaven like? Do you have a paper that says?"

The Lord had given us another chance to tell her that He was not the same as the sun, and we took advantage of it. "Heaven is a beautiful place. In Heaven even the sun isn't needed because God Himself lights our way."

With the phrase, "the sun isn't needed," a queer expression flickered across her face—had the message reached home at last? But she shook back any doubt about her god and said firmly, "Father Sun is taking care of us. We wouldn't be able to walk if the trail were wet and slippery, but we have a dry trail today!"

We parted, Sarah and I heading for home, and the old lady going to a village two hours beyond Rio de Flores. The Lord wanted His Word carried to that remote village, and this time His messenger was a nonbelieving, illiterate woman. We hoped that someone would read the booklet to her, and that he and others there would understand and believe on the Lord.

But suppose they had trouble reading it? Suppose they weren't able to make out its message? Then, even with Scripture in their hands, they still would not have heard. And "How shall they believe in him of whom they have not heard?"

Sarah and I were concerned, not only for Rio de

Flores, but also for other towns where a few people had carried a bit of Scripture; were they reading it? We thought of the town of San Marcos, and we wanted to live there and teach the people to read and understand the Scriptures. Living among them we'd know the people, and could pray for them as individuals. But there were many Mazatec villages; was San Marcos more important than the others? We decided that we'd go and stay until we were sure that at least a few people could read; then later we could go on to still another village.

We moved to San Marcos and started teaching any and all who paused on their way past our house. One afternoon I held a booklet for a group of about twenty men who studied as they stood outside our window. They didn't come into the house because to do so would jeopardize their independence—outside they could walk away when bored or embarrassed. There was almost continual movement as those interested jostled for better positions, and those who had tired dropped back to become spectators only. They had been to school very little, and even simple words were difficult.

One old man, restless on the edge of the crowd, called out, "Sing!" Mazatec hymns are one of our best means of telling women and children about Christ, but I was reluctant to sing for a bunch of restless men. Uncertain as to what their reaction would be, I kept on with the reading lesson.

At last, however, my conscience pricked me. Illiterate, the old man had no interest in reading, and he was waiting only for the songs. The next time he called, "Sing!" I put down the book and said, "O.K.; let's sing."

As I opened the hymnbook, the old man pushed through to the front row. I sang, pointing to the words of the song as I did so. The men didn't become rowdy as I had feared; rather they were quiet, listening.

The hymns, "Jesus Saves," "Nor Silver nor Gold," "My Sins Are Blotted Out I Know," satisfied the old man; so I picked up the First Epistle of John and read from the second chapter. After reading a verse I explained it, or restated it in other words. "Jesus is the One who intercedes for us with God. He is able to intercede for us because He has already paid our sin bill. When He died, it was to pay for badness, for He had no badness of His own."

The attitude of the men indicated that the old man was a recognized leader; they let him ask the questions, but they were alert for the answers. "Jesus didn't stay dead. He was in the grave only three days, and then He came to life again. He is in Heaven now, and He will save us if we ask Him to."

The old man had apparently pondered his next question a long time, "Does the cross hear us when we pray?"

His question startled me, but I recognized it as part of the mix-up between their pagan religion and that superimposed by their Spanish conquerors. From the Spanish conquerors they had learned the name of the Lord, but not His nature. Confused, they had deified the cross. In that character the cross had become part of their daily lives—in order to protect workers from accident they set up a cross before building the walls of a stone house; a cross in a home supposedly protected it from fire.

I was aware of this attitude when I answered the old man. "No, the cross doesn't hear. A cross was the method used by the people to kill Jesus. A pistol kills people but it couldn't hear if we prayed to it, and neither does the cross. It's Christ who hears; He is the One who helps us!"

"Thank you!" said the old man, and I got the impression that all his questions had been leading up to that one. The other men, too, seemed to feel that the lesson had reached a conclusion; and perhaps they recognized the importance of the information received, for before leaving each said an individual "Thank you."

Such opportunities to teach the San Marcos people thrilled us; but we couldn't forget that other villages were still waiting, and that the people of those villages might respond as favorably as those of San Marcos if they but had the chance.

In the hope of reaching those from distant towns, we frequently sold books in the Chalco market. That was one place where people from many different villages could be contacted all in one day. Because Chalco was the commercial center of the region, people walked as much as ten hours, or came the same distance on horseback, in order to buy and sell there.

When we entered the market with our books, people sometimes crowded around, all wanting immediate attention. We'd hand out books for the impatient ones to look at, while we read sample parts to some of the others. We had to read upside down, of course, because those buying wanted to see the page right side up, but they could not read well enough to make a choice without our help.

We had to keep at least half an eye, and half our attention, on things other than what we were reading. In the crowd that surrounded us, some were reading books that they had already paid for, but they were staying around for help over any hard words that might turn up. Other people were "just looking" at books they had not yet paid for. They were all strangers to us, but we had to remember which was which. Unless they thought we were watching, one of those who was "just looking" would slip the book in his pocket and walk away without paying. If we made a mistake and called back someone who had already paid, he was insulted and we had made a potential enemy.

Usually some who came to us were glad for the opportunity to buy something which told about the Lord. Others were not interested in Scripture, but they were thrilled that books had been written in their language. Others liked the diglot books which would help them to learn Spanish. Still others were glad for an excuse to read aloud and to demonstrate to the crowd their superior education.

Each type had to be handled differently, and we tried to place them in their proper category by noticing how they pushed through the circle toward us.

Whenever our selling for the day was over, it was satisfying to remember the books sold, and people from various villages who had bought them. But while we were actually in the midst of it, selling was just plain hard work.

At least once each market day morning, I'd take a rest from the aggressive people by smiling at some shy woman and suggesting that she look at one of my books. Almost any woman in Mazatec dress would answer, "But I can't read."

"It doesn't matter," I'd tell her; "just look." Then I'd open a primer and read a page or two. Most were pleased to see that in the pictures the women were dressed in the Chalco costume. They chuckled when I read the sentence, "My mother has a water jug." Their chuckle was one of delight that any-thing as erudite as a book could speak of something as common as a water jug.

One morning the woman I had selected smiled back, and fell into conversation with me. Her dia-lect told me that she was not from Chalco, and I tried to remember which towns spoke with her type of accent. When I asked, she told me that she was from Avitla, a town about eight hours from Chalco, and a place where neither the Cowans, nor Sarah, nor I had ever been.

Soon another woman joined the conversation, and together they discussed which of the easier books they should buy. I knew why they were buying; it was not for themselves, but for someone back home. According to Mazatec custom, anyone who goes on a trip should take little gifts back to his friends at home. As travelers they realized that the books would make nice gifts, for they were not heavy to carry, and yet they were new and different.

Then I noticed that three men were listening and

occasionally putting in a word. They were too polite to take the conversation away from the women, but they did prompt them to ask what else I had. I pulled out the book of Acts and they immediately liked it. Somebody back home could read, and they wondered which of the Scriptures he would like best. To help them decide, I read them a little from Acts, then from Mark, and First John, and told them some of the high points of each one. That was one of the reasons I liked to sell books; it offered beautiful opportunities to tell even complete strangers of Christ.

Of course, we were in the middle of a crowded market, and people were bumping us with their baskets as they passed, but our new friends were listening so intently they didn't seem to notice. Finally they decided to buy First John. Probably they chose that one because it talked about Jesus and yet did not cost as much as Mark or Acts.

Before we separated they invited me to visit them in Avitla, and that was just what I wanted to do. I wanted to go with them and help them to read and to understand their copy of First John. As far as I knew, it was the first bit of Scripture to enter that town. Mazatec is hard to read, and I wondered if they'd be able to make it out by themselves. Parts of the First Epistle of John are difficult for even those of us with a Christian background; how could I expect them to understand as they struggled through the book alone?

But Eduardo had understood and with very little help from us. Couldn't we expect the Lord to help the folks in Avitla, too? The Lord purposed to help;

He would "have all men to be saved"; and He had said: "I will pour out my spirit unto you, I will make known my words unto you."

Alone? Those people taking the Scripture back to Avitla would not be alone, for the Lord would help them.